# Personal Enc

For Eileen and Charlie Whitby,
with all good wishes from
the author. Bryan Samain

Halesworth, Suffolk. April 2000.

ounters

# Personal Encounters

## Dealings with the Famous, the Adventurous and the Otherwise Exceptional

### Bryan Samain

*Bryan Samain*
*1/2000*

The Pentland Press Limited
Edinburgh • Cambridge • Durham • USA

© Bryan Samain 2000

First published in 2000 by
The Pentland Press Ltd.
1 Hutton Close
South Church
Bishop Auckland
Durham

British Library Cataloguing in Publication Data.
A Catalogue record for this book is available
from the British Library.

ISBN 1 85821 738 5

Typeset by CBS, Martlesham Heath, Ipswich, Suffolk
Printed and bound by Antony Rowe Ltd., Chippenham

To Helen and our families

# THE AUTHOR

1925: Born in Chelmsford, Essex. Subsequently educated at Royal Masonic School, Hertfordshire.

1941: Started career in newspaper journalism. Worked in Fleet Street on *Daily Sketch* and *Sydney Daily Mirror.*

1943: Volunteered for war service. Lieutenant, Royal Marines. Operations with Commando units, 1944–46. Europe and Far East.

1946: Returned from Far East to *Sydney Daily Mirror*, London.

1948: Entered PR. Specialised in industrial public relations and publicity. Worked for several international companies over 40 years, notably British Steel, Cementation, Ford and EMI. Undertook publicity assignments worldwide, in USA, Canada, Middle East, India and Japan. Also in UK and mainland Europe.

Author of *Commando Men*, first published 1948 and re-published 1976 and 1989. Former publicity adviser to The Duke of Edinburgh's Award Scheme and The Save the Children Fund. Director of Public Affairs, EMI, 1970–79. Independent publicity consultant and writer from 1980 onwards.

Now a grandfather with a grown-up family and two grandchildren. Lives with his wife in Suffolk. Devotes most of his time to writing and community work.

# INTRODUCTION

In forty years or so of working around the world, mainly as an industrial publicist, I've had the opportunity to meet a good many interesting and unusual people – famous and otherwise. The sketches in this book are based on my personal impressions of some of them.

Bryan Samain

# CONTENTS

# ROYALS

Earl Mountbatten of Burma

Prince Philip, Duke of Edinburgh

The Dukes of Kent, Father and Son

# EARL MOUNTBATTEN OF BURMA (1900 – 1979)

## A Threefold Greatness

To me, he was a man of threefold greatness. A great-grandson of Queen Victoria, he entered Dartmouth as a boy and went on to become not only a distinguished naval officer but also one of the most renowned Allied military leaders of the Second World War. In 1947, when he wanted more than anything else to resume his naval career, Clement Attlee persuaded him to become the last Viceroy of India and to oversee the transfer of power after two hundred years of British rule. He was born into greatness, he achieved it in his own right, and later still in life he had further greatness thrust upon him.

He was inevitably a controversial figure, with critics and enemies in high places, most of them jealous of his Royal connections and his glamorous, winning public style. There were those who variously described him as arrogant, abrasive, an autocrat, a smoked-salmon socialist, a showman who liked nothing better than dressing up. (Even Attlee once reputedly remarked: 'Rather a Ruritanian figure, don't you think?')

He was certainly obsessed with uniforms, medals and decorations. And he could be overly fussy about minute details of ceremonial that ought not (indeed would not, in the final analysis) concern him. In his last years, living in a form of enforced retirement at Broadlands in Hampshire, and with nothing very much to do, he was given to telephoning officials in Whitehall quite frequently – in order to check and re-check details of the order of procession for the State funeral already planned for him. He also concerned himself closely with arrangements

3

for the funeral service to be held in Westminster Abbey, including seating plans, doors for people to enter and leave by, timings, and so on.

He never suffered fools gladly, as those who worked for him in any capacity would readily testify. The thousands of ordinary men and women who served under him in wartime, however, for the most part hero-worshipped him – and in old age continued to do so.

My own first glimpse of Mountbatten came on a February day in 1946, when he boarded the troopship in which I was sailing with my unit to Hong Kong.

He came aboard at Colombo, where we had made a brief stop. Dressed immaculately in crisply laundered white naval uniform, he moved swiftly ahead of a small posse of aides and staff officers scurrying to keep up with him. As soon as he reached the deck on which we were standing he swung quickly up a nearby companionway so that he could talk to us from a convenient vantage point.

He welcomed us as newcomers to the Far Eastern theatre, proceeding to win us over completely by telling us what a great job we Commandos ('*my* Commandos') had done in helping to win the war in Europe. It was a sort of charm-all speech that we felt instinctively he had made to countless other bodies of troops many times before; yet he succeeded in making us feel, if only momentarily, very special. His personal magnetism was exceptionally powerful, and to most of us irresistible.

I did not see him again for several years, and then on a wholly private occasion. Early in 1951 I had been asked by Alan Campbell-Johnson, who had served on Mountbatten's wartime staff and later as his Press adviser in India, to undertake research into a voluminous collection of documents and papers that he was holding on Mountbatten's behalf. The object was to prepare the framework for a book covering Mountbatten's period as Supreme Allied Commander in SE Asia. The book was to be written by Campbell-Johnson with Mountbatten's approval and support.

Over the next twelve months, assisted by my wife, Helen, I worked through all the papers – reading, cataloguing and indexing hundreds of documents that had been stored, for the most part haphazardly, in dozens of box files.

Much of what we read had been top-secret at the time of origin – ranging from notes of high-level discussions on strategy by Mountbatten and his generals to records of meetings with the Chinese leader Chiang Kai-Shek, the US General 'Vinegar Joe' Stilwell, and many other leading figures on the Allied side of the Far Eastern war. We also sifted through page after page of Mountbatten's diaries (not very revealing) together with innumerable copies of signals from Whitehall, the latter in some cases bearing the stamp of Winston Churchill as sender. To our surprise, too, we found several personal letters from George VI, with whom Mountbatten corresponded quite frequently. One of the most revealing from the King contained remarks to the effect that he could fully understand India's desire for independence and that he would be fully prepared to relinquish the title of Emperor of India, and all that went with it, if and when the time came.

Campbell-Johnson was well equipped to write the proposed 'Supremo' book, not only as a member of Mountbatten's inner circle of staff officers in SE Asia Command, but also as a political historian who had published biographies of both Eden and Halifax before the war. His latest book, newly published, was the highly acclaimed *Mission with Mountbatten*, based on day-to-day diaries that he had kept whilst working for Mountbatten as Viceroy and which was already being regarded as important historical source material.

After I had finished my researches into the Mountbatten papers, Campbell-Johnson told me that the Admiral, as Mountbatten was now termed, wished to see me.

A date was set for 11 a.m. on a day some two weeks later, shortly before Mountbatten was due to leave London for Malta and to take up the appointment of C-in-C Mediterranean Fleet. I duly went with Alan to the Mountbattens' house in Chester Street, Belgravia.

We were received at the door by a manservant dressed in blue battledress, the jacket bearing the monogram 'M of B' over the left breast pocket. We were of course expected, the man explained, but Lord Mountbatten was temporarily detained. (He was, in fact, as we later discovered, talking to Field-Marshal Earl Alexander, the newly appointed Minister of Defence, who had called upon him unexpectedly.)

The manservant led us through the hall into the library, a polished, wood-panelled room gleaming softly in morning sunlight. Capacious armchairs, with small tables standing beside them, were casually arranged across the carpeted floor. Most of the tables had collections of carved miniature elephants displayed upon them, each elephant encrusted with tiny precious stones.

A few minutes later Mountbatten entered the room through a concealed door set in the middle of a book-lined wall. He was dressed in a light grey double-breasted suit and smiled broadly as he welcomed us. A waiter appeared and Mountbatten asked us what we'd like to drink. Alan and I opted for G and T, Mountbatten himself for a coffee cocktail.

We settled ourselves in facing armchairs and he plunged immediately into the matter of the proposed book. The title he had in mind for it, he said, was something like *Campaign with Mountbatten* – a title that neither Alan nor myself commented upon. (We didn't think much of it. Privately, as Alan told me later, he didn't want to be saddled with any sort of title at that stage. He wanted the general structure of the book to evolve first.)

As well as describing the course of the South-East Asian campaign, Mountbatten went on, certain major aspects of his immediate postwar responsibilities as Supreme Commander should be carefully explained – for example, the delicate and highly difficult situation he faced concerning French Indo-China after the Japanese surrender.

He reminded us that Indo-China, comprising the States of Laos, Cambodia and Vietnam, had been artificially divided at the Potsdam Conference in July 1945. The Chinese leader Chiang Kai-Shek had been given responsibility for all of Indo-China lying above the 16th parallel, while he, Mountbatten, had been given responsibility for the whole of the country south of it.

The French, however, wanted Indo-China back in their own hands. They had controlled and administered the territory since the 1850s, although they had had to contend with increasing unrest and emergent nationalism. During the war, moreover, their authority had been seriously undermined as a result of the Japanese occupation; and in September 1945, soon after Japan's surrender to the Allies, Vietnam had been declared an independent republic by Ho Chi Minh, the nationalist leader. Subsequent attempts by the French to reassert control of the country had led to fierce fighting, initially in the Saigon area, and a British force sent in by Mountbatten to try to resolve the situation met with only limited success.

Eventually Mountbatten relinquished responsibility for Indo-China and handed it back to the French. As we sat in his library in Chester Street that morning in 1952, the French were still bitterly engaged in fighting the nationalists and had yet to endure their final humiliating defeat at Dien Bien Phu. The long and bloody war in Vietnam had also yet to come.

Neither Mountbatten nor anyone else could have foreseen this relentless powder-keg trail of forthcoming events. Yet perhaps he still felt sensitive about his own role in the affair, and the decisions he had taken at the time of his command as Supremo in South-East Asia. At any rate, he suddenly looked at me and said: 'Well, Samain, that's what I did; what would you have done?'

It may have been the moment of opportunity for the man on the Clapham omnibus, but it was not the moment for me. There was nothing, after all, that I could usefully say. So I smiled politely and said nothing, content to remain listening quietly to his words.

Despite all the preliminary work that we undertook between us, Campbell-Johnson's book was never completed. The original papers and research notes still exist, so far as I know, and may well have been made use of in the writing of Mountbatten biographies by various authors, as well as for the documentary *The Life and Times of Lord Mountbatten*, produced by Thames TV and Rediffusion. Years later, when we met one day for lunch in London, Campbell-Johnson told me that his Mountbatten papers had long since been handed over to Lord Brabourne, Mountbatten's son-in-law. Brabourne had apparently required them for the official Mountbatten archives at Broadlands. He and Campbell-Johnson did not see eye to eye, for some reason, and the book project had been dropped.

I met Mountbatten on two further occasions, both in the 1970s.

The first was at a late-night party held at Claridges in 1974, following the West End première of the Agatha Christie film *Murder on the Orient Express* – a film financed by EMI and co-produced by Lord Brabourne in his capacity of independent film producer.

There was an impressive turn-out for the party. The guest list was headed by Princess Anne, together with Mountbatten and Agatha Christie (a rare appearance on her part, for she did not normally attend such functions and in any case was confined to a wheelchair). Several of the stars appearing in the film were also present, including Albert Finney, who played Hercule Poirot, and Lauren Bacall, who played one of the many cameo parts.

With elaborate courtesy, and perhaps more than a hint of panache, Mountbatten was to be seen at one stage in the evening wheeling Agatha Christie, small and white-haired, across the dance floor in her wheelchair, finally settling her into place at the same table as Princess Anne and himself.

Later in the evening, Helen and I spoke to him. She said how proud she had been to serve on his London staff at Combined Operations Headquarters during the War. He smiled that devastating smile of his and replied, 'Ah, I always picked the prettiest Wrens in those days.' (Exit Helen, floating on air, followed by myself.)

Two or three years after that première I met Mountbatten once again, this time at the Royal Sussex Hospital in Brighton. He was opening a new wing of the hospital to house one of EMI's then revolutionary body scanners. After a brief official opening ceremony, Mountbatten and the rest of us, doctors, medical administrators, EMI representatives and members of the Press, adjourned to the Royal Pavilion for lunch. Just before the meal began I found myself alone with Mountbatten for a few moments. I reminded him of the day in 1946 when he had come aboard our troopship at Colombo to address us, the men of 45 Royal Marines Commando.

He remembered the day very well, he said, then added: 'During the war I sometimes had to persuade people in high places that you Commandos weren't criminals who'd been specially let out of the jails.'

He looked at me smilingly. I remembered the rumours that had circulated once or twice during the war years, to the effect that safe-breakers and other selected convicts had been brought out of the prisons so that their particular skills could be made use of on Commando raids. There may or may not have been some truth in the story, but if there was, I never came across such people – and neither did any of the Commandos I served with.

After our meeting in Brighton, I did not meet Mountbatten again. In 1979 I was one of the millions shocked and stunned by the news, which I first heard on my car radio going to work, that he had been murdered in cold blood by the IRA.

# PRINCE PHILIP, DUKE OF EDINBURGH (1921 – )

## Awkward Questions

Over a period of twenty years, when I worked at different times for two very different companies, namely British Steel and EMI, my responsibilities included handling Royal visits to a number of factories.

The biggest and most important had to do with the official opening in October 1962 of the Llanwern steelworks and strip mill at Newport in South Wales. The Queen, accompanied by Prince Philip, performed the opening ceremony and spent the best part of a day touring the enormous steelworks site – four miles long and half a mile wide. It was considered at the time to be the most extensive tour of a single works ever undertaken by HMQ. The VIP guests from Britain and overseas who also attended, 1,500 in all, included half-a-dozen Cabinet Ministers in the Macmillan Government.

Other Royal visits that I organised were simpler and more intimate in style, mainly for Prince Philip, to various factories at EMI's complex at Hayes in Middlesex. These occasions usually included a lunch for HRH with executives who were acting as his hosts and guides and I noticed more than once what an extremely fast eater Prince Philip was. He consumed his food very rapidly, and people who were his companions at table often found it difficult to keep up with him in conversation.

In matters of food and drink, however, HRH was really rather abstemious. He had, of course, his likes and dislikes. According to his equerry, he did not care for champagne or red wine, he preferred tomato juice to sherry before lunch, he enjoyed a glass of brandy before dinner. So far as food was concerned he did not like oysters and 'preferred not' to be offered raspberries or strawberries.

On factory visits Prince Philip was always master of his brief. This had to be prepared and agreed at least ten days in advance with the equerry; not too long, just three or four typed sheets of A4 paper, but sufficient to cover the company's background, manufacturing operations, particular points of interest regarding the tour, and the names and career details of key managers and other workers whom HRH would meet. The time-table for the tour (as with all Royal time-tables) had to be calculated and agreed to the last minute. If lunch or any other meal was to be included, simple menus were preferred and possible 'lines of conversation' cleared with the equerry in advance.

Although he could display great personal charm, especially when talking to workers on the shop floor, Prince Philip was by no means popular with all directors and managers. This was largely due to his tendency to ask awkward and unexpected questions – he undoubtedly knew a good deal about British industry and its ways – but executives who really knew their business had nothing to fear, in sharp contrast to those who did not. One director I heard about who took HRH on a certain factory tour was allegedly given rather a hard time. 'The trouble with you directors is that you know absolutely nothing,' an irritable Prince Philip was reported to have said when he found that the director concerned could not satisfactorily answer the questions he had put to him.

The Press resented Prince Philip because of the well-known fierceness he often displayed towards photographers. On one occasion, when I was alerting Fleet Street picture editors about a forthcoming visit by HRH to an EMI factory, I encountered marked lack of interest – abusive lack of interest, in fact – in my telephoned invitation to send photographers along. One editor dismissed the event as a 'total non-opportunity' and claimed that HRH was always 'too bloody rude and hostile' to make coverage of such a visit worth while.

Nevertheless, photographers from several national newspapers came along on this occasion, as in my experience they always did. I invariably found, too, that Prince Philip was perfectly co-operative provided everything had been properly worked out beforehand, so that he would

11

know when and where to expect photographers during the course of his visit.

Much as he disliked Press photographers, and prickly as he was known to be, HRH could be extraordinarily tolerant of show business people. I remember attending a Variety Club supper at the Savoy where a number of well-known comedians and other stage celebrities were also present. Most of them were very free and easy with him, one group standing round him after the meal was over and just about stopping short of slapping him on the back as they proffered raucous jokes and wisecracks. He laughingly entered into it all in a most convivial way. Perhaps the fact that he had earlier been presented with a large cheque from the Variety Club for one of his favourite charities had something to do with it.

# THE DUKES OF KENT, FATHER AND SON

## (1920 – 1942 & 1935 – )

## Gentlemanly Diffidence

I met the present Duke of Kent on two or three occasions in the mid-1970s, as well as his father some forty years earlier. They bore a striking resemblance to each other; both of them tall, sparely built men with receding chins and thin, carefully brushed-back hair; and both of them conveying an air of quiet, gentlemanly diffidence.

The present Duke, in middle age when I first met him, had turned from Army life (he was a major in the Royal Scots Greys) to the world of industry and commerce. Soon after the setting-up of the British Overseas Trade Board he had been appointed its vice-chairman. He was concerned with the promotion of British exports, a job which involved not only leading trade missions abroad but also visiting factories to watch manufacturing at first-hand. He came to two factories operated by EMI, one making CAT scanners in Hertfordshire, the other producing automated lathes in Sussex. I made the necessary arrangements for tours of both, and also escorted him round each of them.

The basic rule for organising Royal visits of this kind, in my experience, was to keep them as simple as possible and avoid unnecessary complications. It was always important to remember that a visitor to a factory, especially a Royal, could hardly be expected to be an expert on what was being shown or demonstrated.

In the case of the Duke, I noticed that he listened with great care and courtesy to everything being explained to him. If there were times when he appeared to wilt it was understandable – particularly if some manager exceeded his brief and went on talking about his work for far longer

13

than he should have done. HRH inevitably maintained his composure, however, and, unlike the Duke of Edinburgh, never asked awkward questions.

HRH's father, the previous Duke, was generally known as Prince George. He was also involved with industry during his lifetime, but in a rather unexpected way and then only very briefly. In 1932, anxious to do something of practical value during the Depression, he was given special permission by his father, George V, to be attached to the Home Office as a temporary inspector of factories. He worked on an unpaid basis for several weeks, visiting factories in various parts of the country. For this purpose he was simply known as 'Mr George' and his true identity was never disclosed. The Press was specifically requested by the Home Secretary of the day to make no mention of his assignment and this was duly honoured. It was a request the media nowadays would certainly ignore, especially as the son of a reigning monarch, the first ever to be allowed to go out to work, was the heart of the story.

My own fleeting encounter with Prince George had nothing to do with industry, however. It arose on a summer afternoon in the late 1930s when he came to my school, the Royal Masonic at Bushey in Hertfordshire, to present the prizes one speech day. For such an important occasion the school had splashed out money on flags and bunting to bedeck the grounds, and for large marquees to be erected to accommodate several hundred visiting parents. In addition, a Royal guard of honour, one hundred strong, had been posted at the main gates to await Prince George's arrival. It was drawn from the school cadet corps, the boys concerned, including myself, ranging in age from twelve to sixteen. We were dressed in pre-war khaki uniforms that included large peaked caps, puttees, and stiffly powdered green webbing with brightly polished brass. Our cap badges and shoulder flashes were those of the London Rifle Brigade, to which the corps was affiliated. Our weapons were ancient Martini rifles with the firing bolts removed.

We waited eagerly for the Prince to arrive, sweating impatiently in the hot sun of an early June afternoon. An hour passed before he finally appeared. He drove up in a black Daimler limousine, and his chauffeur attended him as he alighted. 'I'm dreadfully sorry to be so late,' he was heard to say to our headmaster, who had been waiting with us to receive him, 'but we've been to the wrong school. We lost our way.'

He then walked quickly and silently down our ranks on a token inspection. Rather shyly. His face was covered with brown suntan make-up and his lips bore a faint trace of lipstick. He smiled briefly at me as he passed me by. Nervously, and also briefly, I half-smiled back.

# BUSINESS LEADERS

Sir Patrick Hennessy

Sir Joseph Lockwood

Philip Hofmann

# SIR PATRICK HENNESSY (1899 – 1981)

## Europe's Most Feared Car-Maker

Able and talented people often begin spectacular careers in strange and unexpected ways. So it was with Patrick Hennessy. Born in Ireland at the turn of the century, he served as a young officer with the British Army on the Western Front in the First World War, was taken captive and tried to escape but failed in the attempt. His time as a prisoner left him in poor health. When he returned to Ireland in 1918 he was advised by doctors to undertake hard physical work to build up his strength. He therefore took a job in the Cork factory of the Ford Motor Company, to work in the heat and sweat of the foundries there.

He did not remain long in Ford's lower ranks. He was soon ear-marked as a high-flier and started to soar accordingly. By the early 1930s he had become a key member of the senior management team at Ford's vast new factory complex at Dagenham, built on reclaimed Essex marshland by the River Thames. Responsible for organising the continuous procurement of thousands of different components for car and truck production, he pursued his task with dynamic energy and skill, dealing with hundreds of supplying companies and getting the best out of them at the lowest possible price. His efforts contributed greatly to the successful launch of the Ford Popular in 1935, the only family saloon car ever offered to the British buying public for just £100.

Hennessy's talents as a go-getting manager were put to an exceptional test soon after the outbreak of the Second World War. In 1940 Winston Churchill set up the Ministry of Aircraft Production under the hustling Lord Beaverbrook (a politician and newspaper baron rather than an

19

industrialist) and 'The Beaver' decided in his turn to recruit two experienced, thrustful executives from industry to help him. One was Trevor Westbrook, a former general manager of Vickers Armstrong; the other was Patrick Hennessy, by this time forty-one years old and general manager at Dagenham. Both men were ordered to set about getting results quickly, throughout the aircraft industry. Hennessy's task was to co-ordinate materials requirements and to boost output generally.

The need to do so, at a time when the desperate Battle of Britain was being fought, was urgent; but after little more than a year, thanks to Beaverbrook's ruthless drive and the equally ruthless efforts of Hennessy and Westbrook, the RAF began to receive a greatly increased flow of aircraft. Hennessy then returned to Ford, which was now busily engaged in the production of military vehicles and aero engines. He spent the remainder of the war at Dagenham, and indeed devoted the whole of his subsequent career to the Ford Motor Company.

After the war, having been knighted (KBE) for his wartime services, Hennessy was appointed a director of Ford of Britain. He became managing director soon afterwards and in 1956 was finally appointed chairman, running the company with awesome distinction for the next twelve years, until his retirement in 1968.

I first met Sir Patrick in 1959, when he interviewed me for the vacant post of head of the company's public relations. He sent for me to see him in his West End office – an office above Ford's Regent Street showroom that he used when visiting Central London. He was a formidable-looking man, of medium height, sandy-haired, grave and unsmiling in manner, with pale blue eyes that could suddenly glitter imperiously.

When I first sat down to face him across his desk he studied me silently for a full thirty seconds. I could only gaze back at him in equal silence.

'Talk to me for half an hour about public relations,' he murmured eventually. 'Tell me what you think it's all about.'

I told him what I thought and believed, namely that good public relations were really all about performance. Without good performance, I said, PR was a waste of time because any falsehoods or pretensions would in the end be damningly exposed. Only if a company performed well, in every sense, could it expect to earn a worthwhile corporate reputation – with customers, employees, shareholders, suppliers, and the community at large.

Sir Patrick grunted non-committally. 'What do you consider Ford's present reputation to be, then?' he asked.

'First-class for products, but absolutely awful in terms of labour disputes and strikes,' I said.

His eyes glittered for a moment. 'Well, what do we do about it?'

'Sort out your labour relations, if at all possible.'

Again, he did not comment. Instead, he threw me another question.

'How much do you know about cars?'

'Absolutely nothing, Sir Patrick,' I said. 'I can't tell you anything about what goes on beneath the bonnet. I'm very much Mr Average Motorist.'

Following this interview, I was rather surprised to receive a letter from Ford a few days later, offering me the job. I felt that it was a challenge that I couldn't refuse – I was just thirty-four years old at the time and it was one of the biggest industrial PR jobs in the country – and so I accepted.

I cannot pretend that I had an easy time with Sir Patrick, especially during my first few weeks at Ford, but as time went on I acquired a respect for him as I believe he did for me.

The crunch came when I found that, in his personal dealings with the Press, he tended to favour the *Daily Express*. This was due, of course, to his close personal friendship with 'The Beaver' – a friendship that had begun during the war and now extended to summer holidays at Beaverbrook's villa in the South of France.

Before very long I had various correspondents complaining to me about the favourable treatment that the Beaverbrook Press appeared to be getting compared with their own newspapers. Unable to stop Sir Patrick directly, I resorted to the device, for a couple of days or so, of transferring all national Press calls that we received in my office to his.

'What the hell do you think you're doing?' he demanded eventually. 'I expect you and your people to deal with the newspapers, not me.'

'Then perhaps you could also include the *Daily Express*, Sir Patrick,' I answered.

He glowered at me, but it never happened again, and I noticed that our relationship began to improve from that time onwards.

Ironically, a few months later, in November 1960, the *Daily Express* decided to mount a campaign against the American Ford Motor Company. It arose through Henry Ford II announcing from Detroit that a bid was to be made for all the shares in Ford of Britain that Ford of America, the parent company, did not already hold. (At that time US Ford owned 54.6 per cent of the British company's stock; the balance was held mainly by British investors.)

The *Express* took the view that for Americans to seek to acquire Ford of Britain in its entirety was as heinous a crime as someone trying to filch the Crown Jewels. The company was a major British industrial asset and should remain, if only partly, in British hands. Considerable public concern was aroused by the *Express* campaign, and the whole affair escalated, incredible as it may seem today, to the level of a special debate in the House of Commons, with MPs being asked to vote on the question of whether or not the American take-over should be permitted. Sir Patrick, who supported the American move, was greatly upset by it all – not least because, on the day before the *Express* campaign started, Lord Beaverbrook's son Max Aitken came to see him and tell him that the newspaper was going to do battle against Ford – personal friendships notwithstanding.

Within a few short weeks, however, the Ford Transaction (as the Macmillan Government coyly referred to it in the Commons debate) faded from the headlines. Ford of America paid the then record sum of £120 million for the outstanding shares in Ford of Britain and life at Dagenham resumed as if nothing had happened. Visitors from US Ford's Detroit headquarters came and went as before: in one week, I noted, there were 164 of them, spread across all parts of the 550-acre plant and offices, but this was nothing unusual. Henry Ford II came over, as he normally did, once or twice a year. ('Don't risk his knowledge of your department's workings,' Sir Patrick warned before introducing me. 'Mr

Ford is extremely well informed.')

Yet although Ford of America was Dagenham's ultimate owner, at Dagenham itself Sir Patrick was king. His autocratic style may have incurred dislike but his deep and extensive knowledge of the motor industry commanded widespread respect. If he proved incapable of solving Dagenham's appalling labour relations problems (in fact it took a later management, in a changed economic climate, many years to improve them) then his record as an international car producer took pride of place. In 1960, during my own time at Dagenham, some 3,000 cars a day were being turned out – Consuls, Zephyrs, Zodiacs, Anglias – all brilliantly marketed under his overall direction. It was not for nothing that Volkswagen of Germany reportedly feared Ford under Hennessy more than any other car-maker in Europe. Dagenham was then the biggest exporter of motor vehicles in the world.

On the day of his retirement, 3 May 1968, Sir Patrick received a letter from Henry Ford II which read in part as follows:

Dear Pat: Today, as you step down from the chairmanship, I want to extend my deep personal appreciation for the brilliant service you have rendered the company over many years. You have earned the lasting admiration not only of your colleagues but of automobile men everywhere. Yours has been a most distinguished career . . . and no one will miss you more than I.

# *SIR JOSEPH LOCKWOOD (1904 – 1991)*

## The Man who Saved a Music Empire

I worked under the eye of Sir Joseph Lockwood for several years at EMI. He was chairman of the company from 1954 to 1974, stepping down on his seventieth birthday to be succeeded by Sir John Read, although he still remained a non-executive director.

He was one of the business giants of his day, sitting on the boards of half-a-dozen blue chip companies, serving on Government advisory councils and other bodies designed to aid Britain's industrial performance, a prominent supporter of the Arts. All in all, a commanding figure, widely respected for his capacity to get things done.

During the ten years that I knew him, throughout the Seventies decade, we became good friends only when he had become convinced that I had something useful to contribute to EMI's continuing progress, which was his overriding concern.

However, when I first joined EMI as director of public relations in 1970 he was, I felt, suspicious of me. He had not appointed me himself, John Read had done so as the company's chief executive. To begin with I sensed that Sir Joseph was waiting quietly, and probably none too patiently, to see what I could do.

Several months later, after I had begun to demonstrate that EMI could be effectively publicised as an international pace-setter in electronics, music and entertainment instead of merely being dubbed 'The Beatles Company', which is what the Press and City had called it for years, Sir Joseph began to accept me. One day he paid me a brief compliment and I knew that I had finally arrived. We were sitting alone in the boardroom on the top floor of EMI's headquarters in Manchester Square, London, discussing the story of Nipper the dog in the famous painting called 'His Master's Voice' that was hanging on the wall immediately behind us. 'You shine in your job,' Sir Joseph said to me suddenly. And that, coming from him, was praise indeed.

Lockwood was a formidable and at times intimidating person to many of those who had dealings with him. His physical appearance was one of innate power and authority. He was tall and well-built and had a deep, no-nonsense voice. His fearsome temper was legendary. I was once in his office when, consumed with impatience over a delay in resolving some matter, he made a furious succession of short, blistering telephone calls around the company, all designed to ginger various people up. Then he looked at me challengingly, as if waiting for me to comment. 'I think they're all terrified of you, Sir Joseph,' I felt bound to say, 'but it remains to be seen whether it will really help in getting the answer you're looking for.'

He grunted at the implied criticism. The irony of it was that he was essentially a kindly man, much more so than a lot of people gave him credit for. He was shrewd as well as knowledgeable, too, and a great believer in encouraging anyone who showed promise, especially if they were young and just beginning a career. But he could not bear tardiness. If he wanted something done, he wanted it done damned quick. Everything else had to be dropped in the process. It was the only way to serve him – the way in which, as a young man himself, he had served others.

His career was remarkable, not least because it straddled two entirely different worlds. The first was in flour milling, the second in the world of recorded music, electronics and entertainment. In one respect his business life resembled that of the industrialist J. Arthur Rank who, some twenty years ahead of him, had switched from milling to the film industry to form The Rank Organisation.

Lockwood was born in 1904 in Southwell, Nottinghamshire, into an old-established milling family. He left school at sixteen, trained for three years in the family business, and was then sent to Chile to manage a mill at the age of twenty. He later developed an interest in designing and building flour mills rather than running them, and this led to his return to England in 1928, when he joined the well-known milling machinery manufacturers Henry Simon Ltd of Stockport.

He remained with the firm for the next twenty-six years, eventually becoming chairman and managing director. He travelled abroad extensively, and was internationally recognised as an authority on flour milling. He wrote two textbooks on the subject, one of which became a standard work. Through Henry Simon, Lockwood became a part-time director of the National Research and Development Corporation. This Government body had been set up shortly after the war to protect and exploit British discoveries and inventions. It was chaired by Professor Patrick Blackett, the eminent scientist and Nobel Laureate, who became a personal friend. Lockwood also met the city financier Sir Edward de Stein, who, like himself, was a part-time director of NRDC and, among his many other business interests, a director of the then ailing company Electric & Musical Industries Limited.

EMI was losing money heavily in the early 1950s. It desperately needed a new, vigorous leader to restore its fortunes. Edward de Stein perceived in Lockwood (plain Mr Joe Lockwood as he then was) a man who could fill the bill, even though he had no knowledge whatsoever of the fields of business in which EMI operated.

Understandably, Lockwood was at first not at all keen to fall in with de Stein's pressing suggestions that he should join and re-invigorate EMI. He told me, in fact, that he resisted de Stein's offers and proposals for the best part of a year. Finally, however, he agreed to leave Henry Simon and the flour milling industry so as to enter into EMI's affairs in the capacity of 'part-time try-out deputy chairman . . . but after three or four months the inevitable happened and I took over the place.' It was on 14 November 1954, his fiftieth birthday, that he did so.

Once in full control, and following an intensive study of the company and its problems, Lockwood set about streamlining EMI with a vengeance, slashing costs and driving for greater efficiency everywhere. He never relaxed his efforts. During the lengthy course of his chairmanship he took EMI from near-bankruptcy to levels of performance that more adequately supported its claim to be, among other things, the world's greatest recording organisation.

Lockwood's approach to the art of management was deceptively simple. He believed that a good manager's most important quality was to be able to pick good subordinates and, equally important, to judge accurately what they were really capable of achieving. He was a good picker himself, usually making up his mind about people very quickly whilst interviewing them. He was very tight with money, however, even after EMI had been restored to prosperity, and this sometimes resulted in the loss to competitor companies of talented managers.

His day-to-day working methods were unorthodox, certainly when compared to those of other company chairmen. He would sit at his desk with his personal assistant, William Cavendish, alongside him: in this respect his office was rather like a City partners' room. A woman secretary in an adjoining office dealt with typing and correspondence, but the majority of telephone calls seemed to be handled personally by William and Sir Joseph himself, in that order. Given his ever-present sense of urgency and immediate action, it was perhaps not surprising that he hated paperwork and files, although little (if anything) of significance escaped him. As soon as he had read and finished with written reports he would throw them away. 'I can always get another copy if I need it,' was his basic attitude.

Very soon after joining EMI he demonstrated a natural and surprisingly sensitive understanding of performing artists and their temperaments, and he had a positive gift for establishing friendly relations with them. He got to know most, if not all, of the famous names then current on EMI's roster, and he was as much at home with the Beatles as with Maria Callas. (The Beatles, in fact, seemed to regard him as a sort of father-figure at one time.)

Privately, Lockwood's tastes lay more with classical than with pop music. 'I don't know what Tommy Beecham would have made of all this,' he once remarked to William and myself when the three of us attended a noisy rock concert in North London. As in all things, however, he was a realist. 'The only music I'm interested in from a business point of view is music that sells,' he used to say. He often recalled how he discovered in his early EMI days that classical record producers were revered like field-marshals, but that pop music people were kicked around like lance-corporals. It was a state of affairs that he swiftly and firmly corrected. Pop music, after all, represented 90 per cent of recorded music turnover and profits.

During the years of his EMI chairmanship, and indeed for virtually the rest of his life, Lockwood was closely involved with the performing arts. He developed, among other things, a strong and highly knowledgeable interest in ballet. For a man who had never been to a ballet performance before the age of fifty, he displayed a rapid grasp and acute understanding of the ballet world's creative and administrative needs – so much so that his advice and services were eagerly sought by the Royal Ballet School. He was also persuaded to give time to the needs of the live theatre. He served at different times as chairman of the Young Vic Company as well as the Royal Ballet School, as a member of the board of the National Theatre, and as vice-president of the Central School of Speech and Drama.

He never married. As someone once remarked, he married business instead. Comparatively late in life, he also entered areas of the Arts to which he was instinctively sympathetic and swiftly effective in support. Whatever he engaged in, he was preoccupied with getting results, and preferably getting them fast. He was essentially a mover and a shaker – 'a doer and an achiever', as he liked to describe himself. All of which he undoubtedly was, and to a supreme degree.

# PHILIP HOFMANN (1909 – 1986)

## A Four-in-Hand Chairman

Some people are rightly regarded as larger than life by those who meet and get to know them. I once had dealings with an elderly American gentleman of considerable verve and panache, and not a little egotism, who was certainly in that category. Phil Hofmann was in his seventy-seventh year when I met him for the first time in 1986; he had arrived in England to take part, as the oldest-ever competitor (so he claimed), in the world four-in-hand marathon trials and championships to be held later that year.

Our meeting had come about through a call I had received from the New Jersey headquarters of Johnson & Johnson, the health care company. Phil Hofmann was a former chairman and chief executive of J & J and also a lifelong horseman of international repute. Although his planned participation in the four-in-hand events was not in any way connected with the company's business, it was felt that his story might command a certain amount of Press interest. I was therefore asked to see what I could organise.

Phil Hofmann, I soon discovered, was a big man in every sense; big physically, big and confident in his thinking. When I first called to see him at his Windsor hotel I found him naked to the waist but with a stetson on his head and smoking a large well-lit cigar. He was busy sorting out correspondence and other papers scattered across his bed. It transpired that he had flown in from his farm in Florida a few days before. A specially chartered plane had also brought in two four-in-hand carriages, five horses and two grooms. These were all quartered nearby, as he intended to make Windsor his base during his stay in England. He spoke in a booming, cheerful voice as he welcomed me. Pointing to the cigar in his mouth, he added: 'Meet my trademark. Everybody knows it. I smoke around fifteen a day.'

He seemed in no way deterred by the fact (a fact that I learned only after meeting him) that he was a heart case. Apparently he had had a heart attack when on a visit to India some years before, but this had been successfully overcome. More recently, he had had a triple by-pass operation, the scar of which was clear enough upon his chest.

We spoke at some length about his programme. He wanted first to take part in the forthcoming four-in-hand marathon trials at Brighton, and then similar trial events at Windsor, Sandringham, and possibly Cirencester. Above all, he wanted to compete in the world championships at Ascot, which would take place following completion of the trials.

We discussed various publicity ideas together and then I left him to develop them in more detail. There was no doubt in my mind that he would welcome all the personal publicity I could get: he was an unashamed egotist who had cheerfully made that clear.

In talking to Phil Hofmann, I had gathered quite a lot of background information about him. He was born and grew up in a small town in Iowa, where his father ran a pharmacy. Phil however, was not keen to follow him: his ambitions lay elsewhere. He took a degree at business school, then got a job with Johnson & Johnson as a shipping clerk. The year was 1931, and he was twenty-two. 'In those days of Depression,' he said to me, 'it was a job I was exceedingly glad to get.'

Before long he had the chance of moving to the sales side of the company. Once there, he rapidly made his mark as an energetic, hard-travelling operator, successfully meeting sales targets for a variety of J & J's health care products. Over the next forty years he rose higher and higher through the company's ranks, reaching senior executive levels and eventually becoming chairman – the first non-member of the Johnson family to do so. He retired ten years later, in 1973, to devote as much of his time as possible to horses, his lifelong passion.

Throughout his business career, which was inevitably demanding,

Phil Hofmann managed to maintain an active interest and widespread involvement in the world of horses. Among other things, he instituted experiments in the breeding of hunters – using mares from Canada well known for their jumping ability, and Holstein stallions from Germany, noted for their strength and endurance. The first Holstein brought over to the States under this programme went berserk on the pierside at New York whilst being unloaded from the ship. Rearing and kicking at everything in sight, it sent everyone rushing for cover – with the exception of Hofmann, who advanced slowly towards the frightened animal and succeeded in calming it by talking softly to it in German. On another occasion, ever the born salesman, he drove a four-in-hand with a stagecoach full of people down the length of Broadway to help promote a film première for a New York charity. 'He was,' a friend remarked of him, 'one hell of a character.'

Three weeks after his arrival in England, Phil Hofmann had a heart attack which put him into hospital. It might well have been foreseen, but it was not. His wife, who was staying with him at Windsor, telephoned to say that he was going to have to abandon his entire schedule and fly his horses and coaches back to the States in about ten days' time. She (and of course he) were bitterly disappointed by this sudden turn of events.

I was too. It was not only a question of unscrambling my own publicity plans but, more importantly, a case of a game and determined man – foolishly determined, perhaps – unable to take part in a world-class equestrian event for which in every other way he was supremely qualified. Before leaving England after being discharged from hospital he was privately presented by The Queen with a silver-mounted and engraved riding whip in recognition of his services to equestrian sport over many years. This helped, perhaps, to assuage his intense feelings of frustration because of being forced to withdraw from the championships.

In December 1986, several months after returning to the States, Philip Hofmann died in the Miami Heart Institute. Some time before his death, and before he entered hospital, he wrote to me (game as ever) from his horse farm in Florida, 'I'm afraid, in going over to England, I bit off more than I could handle,' his letter ran. 'The spirit was willing but the flesh was weak . . . I'm sorry our programme did not work out but, as my daughter says, that's the way the mop flops.'

# LAWYERS

## Lord Shawcross

# LORD SHAWCROSS (1902–)

## 'Once, a Kind of Hero . . .'

To many of those who met him in business, myself included, Hartley Shawcross was an enigmatic figure, difficult to imagine as a staunch supporter of the Labour Party in his younger days, as in fact he was. After the landslide Labour election victory of 1945 he entered the House of Commons as MP for St Helens and became Attorney-General in the Attlee Government. He once boasted to Tory opponents in the Commons, 'We are the masters now,' and the implied arrogance of the statement was not easily forgotten, even though he claimed for many years afterwards (with some justification) that his words had been taken out of context. Later in life he became discernibly right-wing, and although he never formally stood as a Conservative he was nevertheless waggishly dubbed 'Sir Shortly Floorcross'.

However, as Sir Hartley Shawcross, QC (he was knighted in 1945) he had a success-studded career at the Bar, starting on the Northern Circuit in the 1920s and swiftly rising in reputation. He handled some of the greatest criminal cases of his day, often as prosecuting counsel, and he could have progressed effortlessly to the highest ranks of the legal profession – Lord Chief Justice or Lord Chancellor – had he chosen to do so. He was widely acknowledged for much of his professional life as possessing one of the finest legal minds in England, yet he ceased to practise at the Bar at the comparatively early age of fifty-six. He was made a Life Peer in 1959 and became more and more immersed in business and commerce. From the early 1960s he sat for over twenty years on the boards of various leading companies – Ford, Shell and EMI among them. He never re-entered politics or practised in the courts.

I knew him when I was at EMI in the 1970s and he was a non-executive director. He was by no means a popular man, at any rate in business, where ordinary souls who had dealings with him found him somewhat remote and condescending. He was nevertheless widely respected for the exceptional power and quality of his intellect. When he was chairman of Thames TV, at that time a jointly-owned subsidiary of EMI, executives who came under his critical gaze and scrutiny at budget and other meetings often found his cross-examining style extremely testing. Howard Thomas, who was managing director of Thames when Shawcross was chairman, described the questioning as 'something to shatter the most hardened nerves' – and Thomas himself was a tough and highly experienced television executive.

In appearance Shawcross was slight and dapper. His voice was quiet, almost drawling. Yet in his utterly discreet way he was something of a showman. A gold-rimmed monocle hung by a black thread across his waistcoat and he would often make great play with it, raising the monocle to his eye and screwing it in with deliberate slowness before carefully examining any document handed to him. He conveyed a clear, almost mesmerising impression of casually analysing the import of the text set before him with deadly accuracy.

To people of my own generation who fought with the Allied armies of liberation across northern Europe in 1944-45, Shawcross was a kind of hero – the chief UK prosecutor at the Nuremberg war crime trials where the captured Nazi leaders in the dock, Goering, Hess, Doenitz and the rest, were finally brought to book. In my own later acquaintance with him at EMI, however, he did not convey quite the same heroic impression. His very presence as a non-executive director, which is what he was from 1965 to 1981, rather puzzled me. He seemed altogether far too distinguished a figure to be sitting on the board of a company which, if only occasionally, was obliged to grapple with the seedier sides of the entertainment business.

This came home to me with particular force during the Sex Pistols/ Thames TV affair which beset EMI towards the end of 1976. Notoriously foul-mouthed and anarchic in behaviour (part of an assiduously fostered punk group image) the Sex Pistols had been newly signed by EMI. It had been arranged by EMI's pop records division that the Sex Pistols would appear on a Thames TV evening chat show – Thames at that time being responsible for the weekday ITV service in the London area. The show's presenter and interviewer was Bill Grundy, who took an immediate dislike to the four punk rockers who appeared before him in front of the cameras. This resulted in an aggressive stream of four-letter language on their part – language that gave rise, in turn, to hundreds of protest phone calls from outraged viewers and a highly critical Press the following morning.

The Press attacks continued over the next two or three weeks, fuelled by ongoing acts of riotous public behaviour by the Sex Pistols. In the end EMI abruptly terminated the group's contract, only to find that another record company promptly snapped them up. So far as EMI was concerned, however, the Sex Pistols affair brought to a head a question that had been brewing within the company for some time – namely what, if anything, could a leading entertainment and media business do to stem the rising tide of obscenity displayed in record lyrics, books, plays, films and TV programmes – all indicative of an increasingly permissive society. Sir John Read, EMI's chairman, who apart from his own personal disquiet was also under considerable pressure from shareholders and others to ensure that EMI was seen to be 'doing something', decided to hold a top-level internal conference on the matter.

The conference was rapidly organised by myself at Sir John's behest. It took place behind locked doors in the Selfridge Hotel (then owned by EMI) in London's West End. Among those present, with Sir John in the chair, were some forty people drawn mainly from the ranks of the EMI Group's directors and senior executives. They included Lord Shawcross; Lord Howe (then Sir Geoffrey Howe, at the time also a non-executive director of EMI); Lord Wolfenden, a part-time director of Thames TV, best known as the author of the 1955 Wolfenden Report on prostitution; Lord (Bernard) Delfont, head of EMI's entertainment operations; Nat Cohen, film producer and full-time head of EMI's film businesses;

Howard Thomas, managing director of Thames TV; Jeremy Isaacs, head of programmes at Thames TV and later to become director of Covent Garden Opera; Leslie Hill, managing director of EMI Records, later to become chairman of the ITV Midlands company Central Television; and Verity Lambert, then head of drama at Thames TV, the only woman business executive present.

To open the conference and set the scene, Sir John asked me to prepare a special twenty-minute video in advance. When screened to the assembled audience, it showed how easy it was for any member of the public, including children, to buy pornographic or other obscene material in any newsagent's shop, and likewise to be able to see or listen to similar material in cinemas, record shops, book stores and elsewhere. The question was: how could EMI realistically combat this on its own, bearing in mind that any material it refused to handle, such as an offensive recording, would find a home with a competitor company and inevitably achieve high sales through notoriety?

There was no clear-cut answer to the problem, and of course there still isn't, but my video at least focused attention upon it and stimulated a vigorous discussion on the part of those present. Lord Shawcross, in particular, spoke out strongly, and in highly condemnatory terms, about all types of obscene material, citing by way of example the film *Emmanuelle* as typifying 'the all too frequent degradation of women' in films and TV programmes. (*Emmanuelle*, at the time, was being screened in EMI cinemas across the country and a clip from it had been included in my video.)

I was so impressed by the force of his remarks that I half-expected him to resign his directorship of EMI once the meeting was over. Had he done so, I think others would have followed his example further down the line. Feelings were running high in EMI over the Sex Pistols affair, with opinions among executives (myself included) sharply divided over the worth of signing up artists like the Pistols – or indeed indulging in any way in the permissive society rat race.

Strongly though he felt on the matter at the time, Lord Shawcross did not again refer to it – at any rate publicly. In his autobiography *Life*

*Sentence*, published in 1995, he made no reference to the conference at all, or to his sixteen-year term as an EMI director, although he referred at some length to his work and involvement with other leading companies.

# ACTORS AND SHOWMEN

Sir John Mills

Gregory Peck

Nat Cohen

Sir James Carreras

Lord Delfont

# SIR JOHN MILLS (1908 – )

## 'The Quintessential Englishman'

To many of his admiring public John Mills is perhaps best known for the films in which he typifies the quintessential Englishman in a wartime setting: the quietly determined soldier, the chirpy yet steadfast cockney sailor, the modest-mannered fighter pilot. I first met him when he was playing a very small part in uniform in *Goodbye Mr Chips*, in his early days as a film actor.

The year was 1939. MGM were filming James Hilton's sentimental story of school life at the now defunct Denham Studios in Hertfordshire. My own school, the Royal Masonic, located at Bushey a few miles away, was providing the schoolboy extras for the crowd scenes – about a hundred of us all told, initiated into the mysteries of film-making over a period of three weeks and enjoying every minute of it.

The main set for the film was a large school quadrangle, overlooked by a chapel, houses and trees. Skilfully constructed, and filling one of Denham's vast indoor stages, it was virtually a replica of the quadrangle at Repton School in Derbyshire, where some of the film's background scenes had already been shot.

One afternoon, after we had spent the morning rehearsing, the director ordered us all to clear the set. We formed a circle round the edge of it, and after a while a young man appeared and made his way towards the centre where a camera and lights had been set up. He was smartly dressed in blazer, flannels and a white open-necked shirt. He stood with his feet planted well apart in front of the camera, hands placed jauntily upon his hips, smiling confidently as he moved his head from left profile to right in response to the director's orders.

I asked an elderly small-part actor standing beside me (he was playing a schoolmaster in one of the crowd scenes) who the young man was. 'I'm not really certain,' he said. 'I think his name's John Mills.'

And John Mills he turned out to be. After the test he was given the part of a young First World War officer, a former pupil at the school, who asks Mr Chips (played by Robert Donat) to look after his wife and baby whilst he is away on active service. He is later killed on the Western front. It was a tiny part, but for Mills it soon led to greater things.

Over the next fifty years or so, I think I saw every film in which he appeared. I also saw him on stage in a musical version of *Goodbye Mr Chips* at Chichester Festival Theatre in 1982. He was by then seventy-four years old and playing the lead. His part required him to sing and dance and to look far younger than he actually was. It was no problem for him: he had, after all, started his professional career as a dancer in a West End musical back in 1929. As Chips he was both believable and loveable.

It suddenly struck me, as I watched him perform, that we were probably the only two people in the theatre that night who had been at Denham Studios forty-three years earlier to take part in the making of the original film version of the James Hilton story. I wrote and told him so, fan addressing star. In his reply he agreed with me. 'What an extraordinary coincidence,' he said. And then, in answer to a question that I had added in my note to him: 'Retire? Retirement is out. I simply can't afford it.'

# GREGORY PECK (1916 – )

## A Film Too Far?

In 1972 Gregory Peck, one of Hollywood's greats, joined EMI. More precisely, he joined the board of Capitol Records, EMI's principal music subsidiary in North America. 'All very well, but what the hell does he know about the record business?' a woman reporter on the *Financial Times* asked me rather sniffily.

Dealing with telephone enquiries that were starting to come in to my office that evening, I was hard put for an answer. Capitol had released a statement in Hollywood that had only just reached me in London. It said things like, 'He brings a sensitivity to the performing areas of the industry which Capitol is very honoured and fortunate to have,' but it did not in any way explain specifically what Peck was going to do.

A few weeks later Peck arrived in London and had lunch in our Manchester Square offices with EMI chairman John Read, myself and several other executives. Although I had long been an admirer of his film performances – in fact I had seen most of them – I found him to be a disappointingly wooden character when I met him face to face. His dark clothes and restrained manner resembled more the cautious banker than the glamorous screen idol. He behaved like a banker, too: his conversation was subdued, at times almost monosyllabic, and essentially serious. He spent most of lunch dropping hints about a film project he had in mind, based on the true-life story of a sixteen-year-old boy who had sailed round the world single-handed. After lunch, when he announced that he planned to fly back to Hollywood that same day, John Read asked him if he would care to visit EMI's record factory at Hayes, on his way to Heathrow. Peck ducked the invitation, but said that he would like to be taken to his tailor in Savile Row before going on to the airport.

Of course, we said. My own car, a Rover 2000, was hurriedly summoned from the company's garage in the basement. Although a grander limousine might have been a better choice, no other vehicle was available. Peck, meanwhile, said his goodbyes and made for the lift. When he reached the main hall on the ground floor he was mobbed by dozens of young women from various EMI departments who had formed a sort of impromptu fan club. He responded immediately to them – smiling, shaking hands, giving autographs – switching on the warm and compelling magnetism of the true Hollywood star.

Outside in Manchester Square, the driver of my Rover stood waiting, ready to take Peck wherever he wanted to go. Peck himself, when he eventually came outside, eyed the car without comment and then proceeded to get in. Aided by myself, he squeezed his large frame into a back seat with some difficulty. 'Are you comfortable?' I asked. He looked at me with a hint of grimness in his eyes. 'I can manage OK,' he said. The car drew away and moved slowly across the Square. It was the last I saw of Peck for some time.

Eighteen months later, in May 1974, the world première of *The Dove*, produced by Gregory Peck with EMI backing, was held in London. It was a typical West End première occasion, not to be compared with Hollywood at its most lavish, but typical then of the British film industry's way of doing things. The venue was EMI's flagship cinema, the ABC in Shaftesbury Avenue. The guest celebrities and VIPs were headed by Princess Anne, and, as most of the evening's proceeds were going to the Army Benevolent Fund, the Army was there in strength too. Welsh Guards formed a 'lining party' in the foyer, State trumpeters of the Household Cavalry provided a Royal fanfare for Princess Anne; a field-marshal and a brace of generals were among the four hundred or so members of the audience. The film industry's representation was headed by Bernard Delfont, John Mills, Wendy Hiller – and, of course, Gregory Peck himself.

*The Dove* is about the adventures and hardships of a teenage American schoolboy, Robin Lee Graham, who during the 1960s spent five years sailing over 30,000 miles round the world in a 23ft sloop of the same name. Despite the strong storyline, hefty launch publicity and a red carpet send-off, *The Dove* was not a resounding success. It did not seem to appeal to the public, and was hardly a financial blockbuster.

Many people felt, and I was one of them, that Peck should not have bothered with the film at all. We all knew him best as an outstanding screen actor who had built up a world-wide following with starring roles in films like *Duel in the Sun*, *Twelve O'Clock High*, *The Snows of Kilimanjaro*, *To Kill a Mocking Bird* and many, many more. We didn't hear much about *The Dove* after its first run through the cinemas, and we certainly haven't heard much about it since. For Peck, perhaps, it was a film too far.

# NAT COHEN (1906 – 1988)

## A Reticent Movie Baron

In his day, back in the mid-1970s, Nat Cohen was the most powerful man in British films. As head of production at EMI he was responsible for all feature film output; at the same time he controlled EMI's film distribution business and, through its chain of several hundred ABC cinemas strung around the country, he also exerted considerable influence on the exhibition side of the industry. His position was therefore unique. He exercised a dominance unequalled not only in Britain but quite possibly in America as well. However strong a Hollywood producer might be, he would not be allowed in his own country, under US anti-trust law, to have such close links with either film distribution or exhibition.

When I met Nat at EMI he was in his sixties and at the height of his career. He already had a lifetime's experience behind him, having first become interested in the film industry when he was in his twenties – through his father, a prosperous East End poulterer, who had an interest in a local cinema.

Nat began by buying his own cinema in Teddington in the early 1930s and progressively developing a small cinema circuit in London and the provinces. He then turned his mind to film distribution, handling re-releases in Britain of Hal Roach and other American comedies. During the Second World War he was concerned with the distribution of military films, but once the war was over he quickly broke into commercial production, making short features cheaply and profitably. (Still remembered by older film-goers, these offerings included Edgar Wallace thrillers and a 'notable crimes' series narrated by Edgar Lustgarten, a well-known barrister and writer at the time.)

In 1958 Cohen came across a story that was to prove the beginnings of a highly successful film idea. He turned the story, a rejected stage play, into a comedy film called *Carry on Sergeant*. It proved to be the first of twelve 'Carry On' films that he subsequently backed – employing the talents of a string of comic actors including Frankie Howerd, Kenneth Williams, Sid James, Barbara Windsor and many others. Though sneered at as cheap and vulgar by his critics, the 'Carry Ons' were greatly enjoyed by British audiences – and by audiences overseas. They also made a good deal of money.

Nat was essentially a businessman whose overriding love was films. He knew every aspect of the film business, watched the trends in the market and studied his box-office receipts carefully – every morning in fact. This did not mean, however, that he was wedded exclusively to the lowest common denominator. Surprising as it may have been to some, he was prepared to back, on occasion, far more creatively ambitious projects than 'Carry Ons' and second-rate features. He financed director John Schlesinger's first major film, *A Kind of Loving*, and backed Ken Roach (whom he once described as 'a genius . . . though I sometimes wish he'd be more commercial') for the making of *The Body* and *Family Life*. He also helped several actors who later became stars, among them Alan Bates, Julie Christie and Tom Courtenay. The most famous production with which he was associated was Agatha Christie's *Murder on the Orient Express*. This featured fourteen international stars, including Sean Connery, Ingrid Bergman, John Gielgud and Lauren Bacall, with Albert Finney playing Hercule Poirot. It gained six Oscar nominations and was an outstanding box-office success. At the time that it was made at Elstree in 1974 Cohen could justifiably claim to be responsible for more than half of Britain's entire film output.

A short, thick-set man with a carefully brushed moustache that gave him a decidedly military air, Cohen was conservative in both dress and manner. He was by nature an individualist, however, and very much accustomed to running his own show. He hated boards and committees (although he was obliged to sit on several at EMI) and within his immediate empire he made every decision on his own – from choosing scripts and actors to settling the intricacies of production finance. He was not particularly interested in personal publicity, rarely gave interviews, and confined his screen credits to the brief introductory line 'Nat Cohen Presents . . .'

Away from the film business, his greatest love was horse-racing. He owned several horses, kept stables, was frequently to be seen at race meetings, and once (in 1962) won the Grand National with his horse Kilmore. He was basically a quiet, rather uncommunicative man, certainly where his own private interests were concerned, and in conversation he was sometimes given to long silences. For a movie baron, he was, outwardly at least, a surprisingly reticent person.

# SIR JAMES CARRERAS (1909 – 1990)

## King of Hammer Horror

Jimmy Carreras was unknown to most of the cinema-going public, but he was the main driving force behind the highly successful Hammer horror films which, from the mid-1950s to the early 1980s, were hugely popular and acquired widespread cult status. I first got to know him after he had retired from Hammer and joined EMI as a consultant. He was then sixty-four.

He was first and foremost a salesman. Not only could he effectively promote and sell films; his range of contacts throughout business was such that he could swiftly develop director-level interest in almost any type of product. He was a small, slightly built, elegantly dressed man with an engaging manner who always seemed completely at ease with anyone he met or had dealings with. He knew the Duke of Edinburgh quite well through his own work for various charities: in fact he was accustomed to telephoning HRH direct at Buckingham Palace (on more than one occasion whilst sitting with me in my office) whenever he felt the need to do so. He would have succeeded effortlessly, I used to think, in achieving whatever he wanted with whatever came his way – even though his attention span was limited. He became quite easily bored, especially after promoting some new idea and successfully enlisting the enthusiasm of others. He preferred them to carry out the actual work and sort out the details rather than do so himself.

Like his contemporary, Nat Cohen, he entered the film business through family interest. His father, after establishing a cinema circuit in London in the 1920s, co-founded a film distribution company, Exclusive

51

Films, in 1934. After the war, in the late 1940s, Jimmy took charge of Exclusive's newly formed production arm, called Hammer Films. During the war itself he served with the Honourable Artillery Company, earning the soubriquet 'Doodlebug Jim' when in command of an anti-aircraft unit helping to defend London. He came out of the Army as Colonel James Carreras, a title he retained for many years afterwards.

From the outset under his direction, Hammer concentrated on low-budget films: these were based initially on the popular BBC radio series of the day, such as *PC 49* and *Dick Barton*, which were successfully adapted for cinema-going audiences. In 1954, following the widespread popularity established on BBC television of the science fiction story *The Quatermass Experiment*, Jimmy acquired the rights and Hammer turned the story into a hit film. This led to the idea of re-working old Frankenstein and Dracula stories and at the same time creating fresh tales of Gothic horror. The first, in 1956, was *The Curse of Frankenstein*. Shot in gory colour, it immediately appealed to bloodthirsty young cinema-goers and became the first of a long line of similar offerings, as well as dozens of other grisly films which bore gruesomeness as their common hallmark. Thus was Hammer ('The House of Horror') born. It lasted some thirty years, producing cult films that proved highly popular in the UK and overseas markets – especially America. It also became Britain's most consistently profitable film company.

Although Jimmy Carreras was chairman and chief executive of Hammer, and very much in charge, there were four other people who made their own particular contributions to Hammer Films' success. They were all creative people: Anthony Hinds, son of Will Hinds, co-founder with Jimmy's father of Exclusive films before the war; Michael Carreras, Jimmy's son, who with Anthony Hinds wrote, produced and directed most of the Hammer productions; and two leading actors who became closely identified with Hammer Horror – Peter Cushing and Christopher Lee.

Hammer's success gave rise to a widespread resurgence of the horror genre, with rival productions being made and various stars appearing in them. 'What a lark it all is,' Vincent Price once murmured to me on the set at Elstree. He had become a popular leading player in horror films himself, and was bizarrely clad in outlandish Dr Phibes make-up and costume at the time.

Unlike his own team at Hammer, Jimmy Carreras was not at all creative, not at any rate in terms of actual film-making. His main concerns were swift realisation of sales potential and a strong bottom line. He required films of the broadest public appeal to be made quickly and cheaply, generally for less than £200,000 apiece. At one time Hammer was making and selling eight films a year, roughly one every six weeks. This output, winning valuable overseas sales as well as in the home market, gained for Hammer a Queen's Award for export achievement.

For all his involvement in the film business, Carreras devoted a good deal of time to fundraising and other charitable work. He was for many years a prominent member of the Variety Club and chairman of the London Federation of Boys' Clubs. He also acted as a special consultant to the Duke of Edinburgh's Award Scheme.

In 1960 Jimmy was knighted and dropped the title of Colonel. Twenty years later he was appointed KCVO, no doubt on account of his Royal connections. 'Come and see me when you're next in my vicinity,' he wrote cheerfully, after his 1980 honour had been announced. 'There'll be a G and T waiting.'

It was typical of his style. I drank what turned out to be a last drink with him in his Portman Square office that day in 1980, but did not see him again as I left the business world of films and entertainment shortly afterwards. In his own way he was, very truly, a star performer.

# LORD DELFONT (1909 – 1994)

## Impresario and Deal-Maker

Despite his involvement in virtually all branches of the entertainment business, Bernard Delfont was more a man of the theatre than anything else. It was the theatre that made him. After working as a performer in the 1920s and 30s – for several years he partnered a girl in a dancing act – he entered theatrical management during the early war years by first acquiring a lease on the Wimbledon Theatre and then seven further theatres in the West End. It was the beginning of a lengthy career as an impresario, during which he presented over two hundred plays and musicals in London, New York and elsewhere.

He was essentially a deal-maker, a persuader with a shrewd commercial eye. When I first met him in his Golden Square office in London in 1970 he was busy talking into two of the four white telephones on his desk with great urgency and enthusiasm. I stood in the doorway, waiting for him to finish, but he released one of his hands from a phone and beckoned me to join him. As I walked towards him he whispered: 'Come in, come in, I've got a lovely deal going here.' In just one sentence he epitomised himself.

I had newly joined EMI at the time. Delfont had sold his theatrical artists' agency to the company some three years earlier and become the main board director in charge of what were then EMI's entertainment and leisure operations. These included film and stage productions, theatre and cinema management, the running of sports centres and large-scale public attractions such as Blackpool Tower. As one of the two most powerful show business figures in Britain (the other was his brother,

Lew Grade) he was frequently sought out by the Press for interviews. Journalists liked him, for he always gave them comment and quotes that they could make good use of. 'I understand them,' he would say. 'I know exactly what they want.'

Because of his dominance of show business and his central role in leading show business charities such as the Entertainment Artists' Benevolent Fund, he presented the Royal Variety Show at the London Palladium for over twenty years. This annual commitment was somehow slotted in with all his other work and involved the organising and cajoling of stars from New York and Hollywood as well as in London. The show often overran its allotted time, once by nearly two hours. A few days afterwards, Delfont was requested to appear before the Lord Chamberlain at St James' Palace where he was informed, gently if rather long-windedly, that Her Majesty might not come to the Royal Variety Show again if her understanding of the time-table was not adhered to. 'I had no idea why the Lord Chamberlain wanted to see me,' Delfont said when he told me the story. 'I thought it might be to give me news of a gong.' (The gongs in fact came a little later. After allegedly refusing a CBE because one of his staff already had one, Delfont was knighted in 1974 and created a Life Peer in 1976.)

Delfont's charitable activities extended in various directions. He ran his own trust and regularly made disbursements to a number of good causes. He would sometimes respond to direct approaches, too – although not always, as a barber who once asked him for some complimentary tickets quickly found out. 'I don't ask you to cut my hair for nothing, do I?' Delfont told him sharply. At other times he could be a great deal more generous, as when I once mentioned to him that a certain young people's charity badly needed more funds. He had lunch with the charity's director and myself and then wrote out a cheque for £10,000 in front of the pair of us over coffee.

Although he was obviously no stranger to high finance and the more sophisticated forms of money-making, Delfont at heart loved simple cash businesses best. To him, coins and notes cascading into the box office or across the counter were more tangible and satisfying than anything else. As the ultimate boss of EMI's nationwide chain of ABC cinemas he would check the cash takes daily, and at regular intervals he would personally telephone cinema managers to see how they were doing – usually at their homes on Sunday mornings. On one occasion, when he telephoned a new ABC manager in the West Country, he got a dusty answer. 'Lord Delfont here,' he announced. 'And I'm Charley's Aunt,' the man replied, banging down the receiver. It took Delfont a further two calls to convince the manager who he really was talking to.

Like other strong-minded supremos, Delfont did not care to be baulked. I was with him one day when some mid-morning mail was brought into his office by his secretary. When she had left the room Delfont glanced idly at the small pile placed on his desk, then picked up the top letter and started to read it, carrying on talking to me as he did so. After a while he fell silent and read the letter again, slowly and more carefully. Finally, as he read it a third time, it was plain that the letter's contents were highly displeasing. He had been out-manoeuvred over some deal or other and his face suffused with anger as he spoke. 'I tell you, Bryan,' he muttered thickly, 'There are villains in this business. Villains!'

He did not explain any further; but quite obviously, diamond had cut diamond.

# INVENTORS

## Sir Godfrey Hounsfield

# SIR GODFREY HOUNSFIELD (1919 – )

## Creator of a Medical Marvel

During the 1970s it was my privilege to head the publicity team that helped to make the pioneering work of Godfrey Hounsfield known throughout the world. He was the man responsible for one of the twentieth century's greatest medical breakthroughs – the invention of CAT scanners. Yet he was not medically trained, he never attended university, and he had only what many would regard as a limited scientific education.

Godfrey came of farming stock. He was born in 1919 on a Nottinghamshire farm and, as he later put it, enjoyed the freedom of an isolated country life. He was the youngest of five children, a quiet, solitary boy who was usually left by his brothers and sisters to follow his own inclinations. Gadgets of every kind, both electrical and mechanical, intrigued him from an early age and he soon showed that he had the makings of an inventor. His enquiring, persistent turn of mind caused him to be fascinated by different types of scientific problem. 'I made hazardous investigations of the principles of flight,' he once recalled, 'launching myself from the tops of haystacks with a home-made hang glider. I almost blew myself up during experiments involving the use of acetylene and water-filled tar barrels – to see how high they could be propelled. In quieter moments I also constructed a primitive electrical recording machine. By such means I learned, the hard way, the fundamentals of reasoning. It was all at the expense of my schooling, where I responded only to the teaching of physics and mathematics with any degree of enthusiasm.'

After leaving school (he attended Magnus Grammar School in

Newark) Godfrey had a brief succession of teenage jobs – builder's draughtsman, cinema operator and radio repairman. When war broke out in 1939 he volunteered for the RAF. He became a radar mechanic instructor, having successfully taken an RAF course in radio, and was posted first to the Royal College of Science in South Kensington and then to Cranwell Radar School in Lincolnshire. 'At Cranwell, in my spare time, I sat and passed the City and Guilds examination in radio communications. I also interested myself in constructing demonstration equipment, such as large-scale oscilloscopes, as aids to instruction.'

His work at Cranwell was recognised by the award of a certificate of merit. It was also noticed by a senior RAF officer, an air vice-marshal who ensured that Godfrey obtained a financial grant to pursue his studies once the war had ended.

Leaving the RAF in 1946, Godfrey went to Faraday House College in London where he read electrical and mechanical engineering for four years and gained a diploma. Then, in 1951, at the age of thirty-two, he joined EMI at Hayes in Middlesex. It was the beginning of what was destined to become a truly brilliant career.

In the early 1950s Electric & Musical Industries Ltd (to give EMI its original name) was engaged in a variety of businesses. First and foremost it was, and still is, in the recorded music business; but its other activities at that time ranged from the manufacture of gramophones and TV sets to a substantial involvement in defence electronics, notably radar, an involvement stemming from the Second World War. Godfrey's initial work at EMI, in fact, was on radar systems. Before very long, however, he became interested in computers, which were then in their infancy. In 1958, as a project engineer, he headed the EMI team which designed Britain's first large all-transistor computer. This represented a major achievement, for the EMIDEC 1100, as it was called, was technically a highly advanced machine, years ahead of any other computer then on the market. Demand for the 1100 was such that EMI eventually built and sold twenty-four for a total of £6 million.

When he had completed his EMIDEC assignment, Godfrey transferred to EMI's central research laboratories at Hayes and found himself once more involved in computers. He worked for several years on a large-scale computer memory project and then, in 1967, began to explore various aspects of automatic pattern recognition – at that time a purely theoretical science which envisaged computers as being able to recognise and identify images as quickly and efficiently as the human eye and brain.

Arising from his research in this area, Godfrey conceived the idea of harnessing X-rays to computers. This highly innovative concept formed the basis of his subsequent inventions of both brain and whole body scanners. They gave birth to an entirely new branch of medical science – computerised axial tomography, or CAT for short.

By providing, on a linked computer screen, detailed X-ray pictures of 'slices' of the human brain and body, Godfrey's scanner yielded information of a kind never seen before . It was to prove a revolutionary means of medical diagnosis, causing doctors, once they had grasped its full implications, to throw away their textbooks and start all over again.

However, because it was so revolutionary, Godfrey had considerable difficulty in getting his idea off the ground. The medical profession, extremely conservative in the main, seemingly had little or no confidence in the idea when it was put to them – and in the case of at least one medical professor, no confidence whatever in computers.

Godfrey made contact with officials at the Department of Health and Social Security and talked at length with them. The DHSS appointed a leading bone radiology specialist to review, independently, the entire new scanner concept. His conclusions strongly supported it and the DHSS eventually agreed to offer backing as well as EMI. Godfrey and his two research assistants constructed a prototype scanner – a crude lash-up affair, built on the bed of an old engineering lathe with bits and pieces of gear gathered from various sources – and made experiments, first with the heads of dead cattle, and later with a preserved section of human brain. The resultant X-ray pictures showed progressively more and more promise as work proceeded over many months. Eventually, in the autumn of 1971, it was felt that the time had come to test the scanner on a living person.

Through the DHSS Godfrey met Dr James Ambrose, a clinical radiologist at Atkinson Morley's Hospital in Wimbledon. The two men took to each other and soon formed a close working relationship. It was arranged that the initial tests on human beings would be undertaken at Atkinson Morley's; and for this purpose an improved prototype was built and installed in the hospital.

The first patient to be scanned was a woman already diagnosed as having tumour of the brain. The scan itself took only a few minutes, but the processing of the resultant X-ray information took many hours. The final pictures, however, convinced Ambrose that they represented a definite breakthrough: the woman had a cystic tumour in her left frontal lobe that could not possibly have been detected unless costly investigative surgery had been undertaken. Ambrose and his medical colleagues were delighted and excited by the scanner's performance.

Further tests on patients resulted in better and better head scans. The time taken to process the resultant pictures was also dramatically improved. The DHSS agreed to purchase the first five machines to be built, for use in British hospitals, and so the stage was set for the news of Godfrey Hounsfield's momentous invention to be broken to the world.

The EMI brain scanner, as the new machine was now called, was publicly launched in April 1972 with a presentation by Godfrey and James Ambrose to an audience of British radiologists. This was followed by a Press conference. The radiologists were reported to be flabbergasted. The Press, possibly because it could not fully comprehend the magnitude of Godfrey's invention, took rather longer to respond. A few months later, in the summer of 1972, Godfrey whetted the appetites of radiologists in New York. Together with Dr James Bull, a leading London neurologist, he presented a series of lectures there on CAT scanning. Then, in November 1972, came the annual convention in Chicago of the Radiological Society of North America. Attended by 2,000 doctors and radiologists from all over the USA and Canada, and also from various other parts of the world, the excitement generated when James Ambrose showed the results of the clinical trials knew no bounds. Hospitals and medical clinics throughout North America, as well as in Japan, Germany and other countries, started to clamour for EMI brain scanners. They all wanted them, and as soon as possible.

No doubt because profits from the new scanner invention had yet to show in EMI's balance sheet, City awareness of the importance of what was happening was still not strongly apparent. In the medical world, however, the soaring excitement in North America literally travelled back to Britain across the Atlantic. Increasing numbers of doctors and radiologists flew in to Heathrow from the States, to inspect personally one of the few EMI scanners then available at Hayes. Initial production of the machines was slow, delivery times of six months or so were being quoted, but this in no way deterred the new customers.

Godfrey himself, meanwhile, was rightly beginning to be recognised by the outside world for his great achievement. The first of what was to become a lengthy list of honours and distinctions over the next few years was made in 1972, when his invention won for EMI and himself the MacRobert Award consisting of £25,000 and a gold medal. He received it, as he did all subsequent awards made to him, with his customary modesty. A diffident bachelor of frugal habits, he seemed largely uninterested in personal possessions, his mind constantly immersed in the complexities of his work.

The scanner continued to climb from one level of success to another. Orders flowed in from hospitals and clinics all over the world, as well as from North America, and a fast-moving medical business – an entirely new business for EMI – was beginning to make a substantial contribution to profits. In 1974 Godfrey, whose ever-restless mind and researches had been exploring further possibilities, announced that whole-body scanning was feasible. A prototype machine was accordingly made to undertake tests and in 1975, at an international symposium of radiologists in Bermuda, Godfrey showed the first results. They consisted of 'slices' of his own body obtained by scans made under laboratory conditions at Hayes. The audience burst into spontaneous applause, although Godfrey himself was as modest as ever when he showed them.

The year 1975 marked a high point in the CAT scanner story. The news of Godfrey's latest invention spread like wildfire through the international medical profession. In London *The Times* newspaper ran a front-page story emphasising the importance of Godfrey's work. The international media immediately followed this up, and over the ensuing weeks a flood of Press, radio and TV enquiries ensued. The City and Wall Street got excited too, with investment analysts and brokers scenting ever-greater profits to be made, so that EMI shares became (temporarily, at least) the hottest property in the financial markets. One Wall Street analyst flew in specially to Hayes, spent thirty minutes looking at the prototype body scanner and asking one or two questions, then flew back to New York to recommend a strong 'buy' of EMI stock.

Soon after Godfrey's sensational demonstration at Bermuda, moves to step up production of both types of EMI scanner got under way. In Britain, output at Hayes was supplemented by the opening of a new factory at Aldenham. Overseas, because the United States had always been rightly perceived as the world's wealthiest and most responsive medical market, plans to establish a factory for EMI scanner production, on a site just outside Chicago, were also put in hand.

It was at this point, however, around the middle of 1976, that the bandwagon started to hit commercial and political problems. Although orders continued to roll in to EMI for both types of scanner, competitors were beginning to emerge. Despite the worldwide patenting of Godfrey's invention, foreign companies in the medical electronics field were in no way deterred from launching scanners of their own – having by now got to grips with the new technology.

Even more ominously, following President Carter's election in 1997, the United States Government decided to embark upon a programme of health-care cost containment under which expensive body scanners, however effective, became the prime target. Orders in the US started to decline sharply as a result. Elsewhere in the world, notably in Japan, the UK and mainland Europe, orders were still being well maintained but could not match the volume being lost in the USA.

EMI was also beginning to experience difficulties in other directions. Its worldwide music operations ran into a sudden downturn – the victim of a major recession in the recorded music business. Combined with the deteriorating EMI Scanner situation, where mounting costs in the USA were also seriously affecting profitability (the Chicago factory never really got going), EMI as a company suffered a double blow from which it did not recover. Within three years, by 1980, it had been forced to withdraw completely from medical electronics operations and to sell its Scanner interests to competitors.

The extraordinary abruptness of EMI's departure from the world medical scene nevertheless could not detract from its earlier achievements in successfully launching CAT scanners on the market – let alone from the pioneering achievements of Godfrey Hounsfield himself. Over a period of five years, from 1972 to 1977, EMI sold just over 700 brain and body Scanners to hospitals and clinics in thirty countries – the majority, 460, to the United States.

Godfrey, in the meantime, became rightly famed and honoured. He was made a Fellow of the Royal Society in 1975, appointed CBE in 1976 and knighted in 1981. Academic honours were showered upon him: between 1972 and 1980 he was the recipient of six honorary degrees from universities and more than forty prestigious awards by scientific institutions throughout the world.

In 1979, he also became a Nobel prizewinner. He shared the award with an American physicist, Allan MacLeod Cormack, who had pursued independent research into the theory of computerised tomography at Tufts University in the mid-1960s. Godfrey was completely unaware of Cormack's work in the same field, as the Nobel authorities officially acknowledged. The two men received the prize for 'the development of computer-assisted tomography'. Godfrey's own work was described in the Nobel citation as 'epoch-making in medical radiology . . . with an unusual combination of vision, intuition and imagination, and with an extraordinarily sure eye for the optimal choice of physical factors in a system that must have offered very great problems to construct, he obtained results which in one blow surprised the medical world. It can be no exaggeration to maintain that no other method within X-ray diagnostics has, during such a short period of time, led to such remarkable advances.'

The news of Godfrey's Nobel award first reached EMI in a rather surprising fashion. I was sitting in my office late one October morning in 1979 when the phone rang and a man on the Associated Press news desk in New York spoke to me. He said that the AP office in Stockholm had heard unofficially that Godfrey Hounsfield was the joint winner of a Nobel Prize: could I confirm it? I said I couldn't. I did not think that anyone in EMI knew anything about it, and rang off. Immediately afterwards I quickly organised some enquiries within the company and it appeared that indeed we did not know anything about it. However, after representations to Stockholm, the Nobel Foundation put out a statement later that day confirming that the 1979 Nobel Prize for Physiology or Medicine (to give the formal title) had been jointly awarded to Allan Cormack and Godfrey.

With the official breaking of the news we had to move fast, as always in the news-handling business. Press enquiries started to flow in during the afternoon and Godfrey had to be contacted – to ask if he would be prepared to give an immediate Press conference. He agreed, and within an hour or so we had science correspondents from national newspapers, news agency reporters, overseas correspondents based in London, and a complete CBS TV crew who wanted the story for New York – all assembled in a central London hotel. Godfrey himself, when he appeared, was as relaxed and courteous as ever, but obviously a little tired. He answered all questions put to him with great patience, explaining to the uninitiated how a CAT scanner worked and, in more personal terms, what he would do with his share of the Nobel prize money. ('I shall equip a room in my house,' he modestly told a *Daily Express* reporter, 'and potter about with interesting ideas. It's my hobby.')

I have a final recollection of Godfrey at the conference. I was listening to him talking to a *Daily Telegraph* correspondent about the hundreds of letters he received from people all over the world whose illnesses had been successfully diagnosed by his scanner inventions. 'I get regular letters from patients,' he said, 'and it's one of the greatest bonuses of my work.'

# AUTHORS AND DRAMATISTS

Stephen Potter

Sean O'Casey

# STEPHEN POTTER (1900 – 1969)

## Exponent of a Gentle Art

People used to describe Stephen Potter as the funniest man they'd ever met but couldn't remember anything he'd actually said. By common consent he was a man of great wit and personal charm. He was also a brilliant impromptu speaker and a comic writer with unusual powers of invention. He coined the terms Gamesmanship, Lifemanship and One-Upmanship ('the gentle art of demoralising opposition') which formed the subjects of three of his most successful books. He gained widespread fame in his day, and not a few imitators.

He was a long-standing friend of Howard Marshall, the broadcaster and public relations expert. They first met up at Oxford and later became colleagues at the BBC, where Potter was a radio producer. They were also fellow clubmen at the Savile. One day Howard brought Stephen back from lunch and introduced me to him. I was working with Howard in Brook Street at the time (it was around 1954) for Richard Thomas & Baldwins, the steel company, and my responsibilities included the editing of a monthly newspaper for 20,000 steelworkers.

Howard thought that Potter might usefully contribute a regular humorous column to the newspaper, and suggested to both of us that we might like to discuss it. Potter and I adjourned to my office accordingly and there, with great earnestness, we kicked Howard's idea around. Potter seemed very keen, but I was not so enthusiastic. I did not feel that Gamesmanship and Lifemanship were themes that would readily strike steelworkers as blindingly funny and in the end I said to him, 'I just don't think the idea will work. Steelworkers, in my view, don't have your sort of humour. I sometimes feel, in fact, that different types of humour present far greater social barriers than we realise.'

'Good heavens,' Potter replied, with an absolutely serious face. 'That's a most profound remark. May I quote you in my next book?'

We did not go ahead with the humorous column idea, and I certainly do not think Potter ever quoted me anywhere. Whether he one-upped me, or I one-upped him, is a matter of conjecture. (Potter's biographer, Alan Jenkins, to whom I related the story years later, clearly thought that I had won. But I was by no means so certain.)

# SEAN O'CASEY (1884 – 1964)

## Casting a Magical Spell

My encounter with Sean O'Casey was strange and fleeting. It arose through two mutual friends, Jack and Mina Carney. Jack was a tough, cigar-smoking Irish-American newspaperman with whom I worked as a teenage reporter on the London staff of the *Sydney Daily Mirror* in the early years of the war. Mina, his American wife, was a sculptress. They had both known O'Casey since his Dublin days, back in the 1920s.

Jack and Mina 'took me up' as a youngster, encouraged me in my work, and often invited me in for drinks in their Fetter Lane flat, which was conveniently close to the *Sydney Mirror* office in Fleet Street. Later, when I volunteered for the Marines in 1943, they kept in touch with me throughout the months I spent in Devon as a recruit and subsequently at officer training school. The O'Casey family lived in Totnes at the time, and Jack and Mina saw to it that I was given a suitable introduction. I was duly invited to tea at Tingrith, the O'Caseys' rambling old Victorian house near Totnes station, and I gladly made the pilgrimage. On arrival I was welcomed by Eileen O'Casey and Breon, their eldest son.

The O'Casey household, as I remember it, was one that could be clearly divided in one's mind. There was the 'family' part, dominated by the beautiful, vivacious Eileen: very homely, very English in character, even though Eileen herself had been born in Dublin; her years on the West End stage had clearly made their mark. Then there was old Sean's part of the house, or rather his secluded study, reverentially treated by the rest of the family, a great tobacco smoke-filled den of a place, the walls racked with untidy rows of books, and an ancient table in the middle of the room, strewn with papers surrounding an equally ancient Oliver Number Nine typewriter.

Sean himself, pipe in mouth and scrabbled white hair wreathing his head like a halo, received me cautiously, a young eighteen-year-old subaltern in freshly pressed uniform, newly commissioned with one pip on each shoulder, highly conventional and disciplined. To a casual onlooker we would probably have made a rather strange pair. Here was the ageing, sixty-ish, mettlesome Irish dramatist, world-renowned, the man who made 'golden embroidery out of dancin' words', meeting a young, eager but rather awkward English boy, obviously Conservative if anything at all, and him a communistically-inclined, free-mouthin' poetic sort of feller stridden from the depths of the Dublin tenements.

But at the time I was very much under Sean's magical literary spell. I was more than familiar with *The Plough and the Stars* and *Juno and the Paycock*; and I had recently devoured two of his volumes of autobiography, *I Knock at the Door* and *Drums under the Windows*, as well as his latest play *Red Roses for Me*, so I had at least some common ground on which to talk to him. He seemed, however, more interested in my experiences as a recruit at the Marines depot a few miles away at Lympstone, and in my more recent officer training at Thurlestone further down the south Devon coast. Perhaps it was because he felt that his own sons would be called up before the war was over, though he did not say so. (In 1946, when I was demobilised, Jack Carney arranged for my Sam Browne belt to be give to Breon, so that he could make use of it when he signed on and hopefully gained a commission. Whether Breon ever wore it or not I have no idea; maybe he still has it somewhere.) At any rate, old Sean and I talked at some length about camp life and other relatively uncontroversial military matters, and nothing else in particular. Later that afternoon we joined the family for a splendid, filling tea, enough to delight the heart of any hungry young solder. And a week or two afterwards, when I wrote to Sean and asked him to inscribe two of his books for me (which he did, in his careful, rounded hand) he gravely advised me that Bryan was acceptable – but never Brian. Spelling my name with an 'i' he said, would have been very wrong indeed, as I have always since remembered.

# SPIES AND SOLDIERS

Maurice Buckmaster

Dudley Coventry

Derek Mills-Roberts

# MAURICE BUCKMASTER (1902 – 1992)

## Spymaster Extraordinary

My friendship with Maurice Buckmaster came about in an unusual way. In 1960, when I knew of him mainly because of his wartime activities, I found myself being headhunted to take over his job as Ford Motor Company's head of public relations at Dagenham. Maurice, it later transpired, although I did not know it at the time, had decided to leave Ford because of a long-standing personality clash with Sir Patrick Hennessy, the company's UK chairman. The two men, in fact, hated each other.

Ironically, it was almost entirely due to his pre-war career with Ford that Maurice gained the intimate knowledge of France and the French people that was to prove so invaluable in the Second World War. As a young man in the 1920s he worked briefly on a Paris newspaper, then, after six years of merchant banking in London, returned to France in 1929 to join Ford's French subsidiary. From 1936 to 1939 he was head of Ford's European department, again based in Paris.

Maurice had a gift for languages. As a boy at Eton he learned French with ease and helped to teach other boys younger than himself. He also became fluent in German. On the outbreak of war in 1939 he was commissioned into the Intelligence Corps and went with the BEF to France. After Dunkirk, where he was one of the last officers to be evacuated, he became a natural candidate for the newly forming Special Operations Executive back in London.

From the start, SOE was a controversial organisation in Whitehall, and no part of it more so than the French section of which Maurice soon became the head. Its cloak-and-dagger role was strongly resented by MI6, who considered SOE essentially amateur and in any case involving itself in matters which were more properly the concern of the Secret Intelligence Service (SIS). After the fall of France, however, Winston Churchill had issued his famous order to set Europe ablaze, and SOE was the direct outcome. Maurice's task, as head of F section, was to recruit suitable agents who could be specially trained and parachuted into France, and also to develop the organisation of a network of French resistance groups.

The task proved difficult for two main reasons. French people escaping from France could not automatically be considered as possible agents; the comparative few who did reach Britain usually joined the Free French movement under General de Gaulle; and de Gaulle in any case strongly disapproved of French nationals being recruited for anything else. On the British side, there was the problem of finding enough people who could speak French like a native – as well as possessing other qualities. Nevertheless, over 150 British men and women were successfully found and trained. Two of the most famous were Odette Hallows and Violette Szabo, both of whom were awarded the George Cross for bravery – Violette Szabo posthumously.

Although Buckmaster and the SOE were heavily criticised after the war for alleged incompetence and lack of professionalism, the fact remains that they achieved notable successes, particularly at the time of the invasion of Normandy, when F section's agents and resistance groups severely disrupted German troop movements – so much so that in the view of General Eisenhower, the Allied commander, Buckmaster's contribution to the eventual defeat of the Germans in France was the equivalent of fifteen divisions of troops. Adolf Hitler, it was also said, regarded Buckmaster as such a menace that he placed him third on his death list.

By the time I came to know Maurice the war was well behind us. He used to take me to lunch at the Special Forces Club in Knightsbridge, a small, intimate place where photographs of wartime agents lined the walls and surviving agents were sometimes to be seen in the bar. Maurice was essentially a courteous and kindly man, and I often thought that he must have agonised a good deal over the fate of many of the people that he sent to France. Over 25 per cent of the four hundred agents who operated under his command were eventually killed by the Germans, many of them after torture. One story that he told me was particularly poignant. A woman agent whom he had recruited and trained in Britain married one of her male colleagues in London shortly before being sent to France as a courier. Three months later, her tour of duty completed, arrangements were made for her to return to England by submarine. She was landed on a Dorset beach by rubber dinghy, and found Maurice waiting for her. 'I had to tell her that the situation had changed and that her immediate return to France was imperative,' he told me. 'It was then that she informed me that she was pregnant, but she agreed to go back. Fortunately we were able to get her out again a little later and she had the baby in England.'

The war left Maurice with a hatred of Germans which never left him. Throughout his time at Ford he refused to visit Germany or have anything to do with the German Ford company. (This was by no means surprising: his opposite number at Ford of Germany, as I later discovered for myself, had been a colonel in the SS.)

When Maurice finally departed from the Ford empire in 1960 he became a freelance public relations consultant. His principal client was the champagne industry of France, which he happily represented in Britain for the next twenty years. The great champagne houses could hardly have picked a better person. With his extensive range of media and other contacts he promoted and protected their interests in this country very successfully and, at the same time, sustained his lifelong love affair with France and all things French.

The sole honour accorded to Maurice by the British Government for his exceptional wartime service was a niggardly OBE. The French, on the other hand, made him an Officer of the Légion d'Honneur, named several streets in various parts of France after him, and continued to fête him whenever he crossed the Channel to visit them. He lived to the age of ninety, spending his last years in a small Sussex hotel, and died in 1992.

# DUDLEY COVENTRY (1915 – 1993)

## Fifty Years a Soldier of Fortune

The true life story of Dudley Coventry – commando, paratrooper, military adventurer and specialist in unconventional warfare – surpasses in many respects the exploits of any fictional James Bond type of hero. For some fifty years, from the late 1930s onwards, he was involved in combat operations, clandestine and otherwise, in Europe, Africa, and the Far East.

Disowned at the age of twenty-two by a wealthy father who apparently despaired of his son's ability to settle down to a quiet and steady business life, Dudley joined the Army in 1938, went to Sandhurst and duly gained a commission. Posted to India soon afterwards, he saw action with his regiment on the North-West Frontier, then found himself back in England. It was during the earliest part of the Second World War, when special service units were being raised at Churchill's urgent insistence to hit back at the Nazi conquerors of Europe. Dudley promptly volunteered for the newly formed Army Commandos and took part in raids on the French coast and the Channel Islands.

He was probably the most perfect physical specimen I ever met; over six feet tall and with a body tapering from strong, broad shoulders to a slim, hard waistline. His face was square-jawed, dominated by a large, sandy-coloured handlebar moustache. His nose was broken and he wore horn-rimmed spectacles. He had once been an Army heavyweight boxing champion and his looks reminded me strongly of the pre-war boxer Len Harvey. Essentially a man's man, modest and somewhat diffident, he was nonetheless extremely attractive to women, among them the film star Ava Gardner, with whom he once had a brief affair.

I served with Dudley during the war. We were brother officers in 45 Royal Marines Commando, one of four Army and RM Commando units comprising the First Commando Brigade. Dudley was a captain, originally from the East Lancashire Regiment, and he had been seconded to '45'. As one of our fighting troop commanders (a fighting troop was roughly the equivalent of an infantry company, although numerically smaller) Dudley took part in operations in Holland and north-west Germany. During a bitterly fought battle against SS troops in the freezing winter snows of January 1945 at Brachterbeek, in southern Holland, one of Dudley's men – a young medical orderly named Eric Harden – won a posthumous VC for his bravery in rescuing three wounded comrades under fire. A few weeks later, after 45 Commando had stormed across the Weser in Germany, Dudley and his men once more came up against SS troops, concealed this time in hedgerows on the other side of the river. During the furious hand-to-hand fighting that ensued, Dudley killed an SS trooper with a single blow of his fist.

When the war in Europe came to an end in May 1945 the Army Commandos started to be disbanded. Dudley accordingly left '45' and we heard little more of him for some time – we were in any event headed for the Far East. Dudley, meanwhile, had rejoined his regiment in India. Two years later, in 1947, he switched to the Parachute Regiment and served with the 1st Paras in Germany, Cyprus and Palestine. By the mid-1950s he had switched again, this time to the SAS, with whom he engaged in counter-insurgency operations in Malaya during the anti-Communist campaign.

After Malaya, to avoid being posted to a desk job, he resigned his British Army commission and joined the French Foreign Legion in Algeria. By 1960, however, he was back in the SAS and serving in Central Africa, a move that was to prove a turning point in his career. Resigning from the Army for a second time, he joined the Rhodesian Light Infantry and became involved with Ian Smith, the Rhodesian Front leader. When Smith made his unilateral declaration of independence in 1965, Dudley helped form a Rhodesian SAS unit designed to combat the black nationalist guerilla movement in that country. His work led to further and deeper involvement in clandestine warfare: in 1970, at the age of fifty-five, after transferring from Rhodesia's SAS to its Central Intelligence Department and ostensibly becoming a civilian, he ran a shadowy operation for ten years which was unofficially known as 'the funnies'. His tasks included the secret training of right-wing guerillas to fight the Frelimo government in Mozambique that had sprung up following Portugal's withdrawal from that country.

When Rhodesia ceased to exist in April 1980 and Zimbabwe emerged as an independent state in its place, Dudley found (possibly to his surprise) that its new black rulers bore him no ill will. He joined the Zimbabwe National Army in the rank of major and helped establish its specialist parachute assault group. Later he was promoted to lieutenant-colonel and given the job of setting up Zimbabwe's own SAS. He continued until the late 1980s to play a leading part in clandestine security operations in Southern Africa, and then finally retired.

After a violent, venturesome life as a soldier, Dudley came to a violent end as a civilian. Whilst asleep at his home in Harare one August night in 1993 he was attacked by a drunken intruder and badly beaten about the head with a rifle butt. Lapsing into a coma, he died one month later at the age of seventy-eight. At his funeral he was accorded full military honours by the Zimbabwe Army. His killer, an unknown man later named as Elijah Chimuchenga, was eventually caught and sentenced to death by Harare's High Court in May 1996.

# DEREK MILLS-ROBERTS (1909 – 1980)

## Commando Leader 'Fiery and Astute'

Brigadier Derek Mills-Roberts, Irish Guards, was an outstanding Commando leader in the Second World War, a man of great personal courage and resourcefulness who gained unqualified respect. Although a 'natural' as a soldier, he was not in fact a professional. He was a solicitor who worked in his father's office in Liverpool and no doubt found it somewhat boring as a young man. In 1936, when he was twenty-seven, he started to take a serious interest in soldiering and joined the Irish Guards as a supplementary reserve officer, spending four weeks in training each year at the Guards' depot at Caterham. Immediately war was declared in September 1939 he was off to join his regiment, taking part a few months later in the short-lived Norway campaign and then, with Commando units being actively formed, volunteering for what was officially termed 'special service of a hazardous nature'.

He was a handsome, well-built man of medium height, with strong wavy hair that was prematurely white. He spoke with a deceptive drawl, for as anyone on the receiving end of his tongue could testify, he was not a man to be trifled with. His basically aggressive character stamped him as a fighter, fast-thinking and equally fast on his feet, who gave no quarter. He was known by all his men as Mills Bomb. 'His withering exterior,' a fellow-officer once observed, 'concealed an amazingly astute soldier.'

By 1942, following tough training and initial raiding experience, Mills-Roberts was second-in-command of Number 4 Commando under the legendary Lord Lovat. Together they led one of the most brilliant Commando operations of the war – the assault from the sea on the German coastal gun battery surmounting the cliffs at Varengeville, on the western side of Dieppe. The attack, which completely destroyed the battery, was part of the large-scale raid on Dieppe mounted by British and Canadian troops in August 1942 which, although yielding valuable lessons, resulted in heavy casualties. The Commando action at Varengeville was later described, in fact, as the only complete and unqualified success of the entire Dieppe operation.

The following January Mills-Roberts was sent to Tunisia to take command of Number 6 Commando. His new unit, by the time he arrived there, had been greatly reduced in numbers – from 600 to 250 men – after heavy fighting. Under his leadership the Commando continued to hold its sector of the British First Army's line and, in one epic engagement, to halt the advance of an entire tank-supported German paratroop regiment. For this achievement Mills-Roberts was awarded a DSO to add to the Military Cross he had already won at Varengeville.

His greatest achievements, however, were yet to come. In June 1944, by now a lieutenant-colonel and still commanding Number 6, he took part in the D-Day landings in Normandy. One week later he became leader of the First Commando Brigade, the parent formation, in succession to Lord Lovat who had been severely wounded.

Promoted to Brigadier, Mills-Roberts subsequently led – with great panache and thrustfulness – the Brigade's four Army and Royal Marines Commando units, some 2,500 men in all, for the rest of the war in north-west Europe. After fighting in Normandy and Holland, the Brigade's exploits included the successful storming of four rivers in Germany – the Rhine, the Weser, the Aller and the Elbe. In the opinion of one military historian, Hilary St George Saunders, its men were among the most expert soldiers that the war produced. Such professionalism was due very much to Mills-Roberts' leadership and his insistence on the highest standards of soldiering and discipline. Anyone who was with him could not fail to be impressed by his exceptional qualities. He was rightly much-decorated, winning a second DSO as well as his MC, and two French decorations – the Légion d'Honneur and the Croix de Guerre.

I served for twelve months under Mills-Roberts from Normandy onwards, in two of the Commando units of his Brigade. His fiery spirit was always in evidence, right through to the end of the war and indeed beyond it.

Early in May 1945, a few days before the signing of the official German surrender at Luneberg, the Brigade found itself at the small port of Neustadt, some twelve miles north of Lübeck. As well as discovering a large concentration camp filled with hundreds of starving and ill-treated people, our Commandos found evidence of appalling atrocities at the nearby beach resort of Travemunde, where thousands of men, women and children had been kept prisoner in the holds of barges and other anchored vessels. All of them had been dragged ashore shortly before our arrival and shot or clubbed to death by their German guards.

Mills-Roberts went to Neustadt and Travemunde to see the evidence for himself. When he had done so he returned to his headquarters in furious anger. Meanwhile a German field-marshal, Erhard Milch, had arrived there and wished to surrender formally to him.

The field-marshal, who held the title of Inspector-General of the Luftwaffe, was one of a party of German officers rounded up by our Commandos and brought in as captives. Milch, dressed in a black leather overcoat and wearing an upswept peaked cap, was carrying his field-marshal's baton – a black silver-headed ebony stick with his name inscribed upon it. As Mills-Roberts approached he clicked his heels together and lifted the baton in ceremonial salute. Mills-Roberts, even more incensed, snatched the baton from him. Shouting 'All you bloody Germans are the same!' he broke it over Milch's head, knocking him temporarily senseless. A member of Mills-Roberts' staff later retrieved most of the pieces of the broken baton, had it repaired, and persuaded him to keep it as a wartime souvenir. Mills-Roberts eventually took it back to England with him and put it in an old drawer, where it lay virtually forgotten for many years. But that was not the end of the story.

When he returned to civilian life after the war, Mills-Roberts resumed practising as a solicitor in Liverpool and finally retired to farm in North Wales. He died in 1980. Five years later it was reported in the Press that the baton was to be auctioned in London. Mills-Roberts' family wanted to get rid of it – one of them was reported as saying that it was 'too evil' to remain in the family's possession. Milch himself, meanwhile, had died in 1972, a convicted war criminal. Before his death he had complained in a book of being assaulted by 'a young British officer' at the time of his surrender in northern Germany.

A few days after the proposed auction had been announced an unexpected legal row developed. The Milch family in Germany, learning what was afoot, argued that Mills-Roberts had forcibly deprived the field-marshal of his baton forty years earlier and that it should therefore be passed to them as family property rather than sold publicly. They instructed a leading firm of London solicitors to apply for an injunction so that the auction could be stopped. This move was contested by the Mills-Roberts family, and in a private hearing in the High Court the Milch family's action was withdrawn. The baton was eventually sold at auction by Phillips in 1986 for £6,800, the buyer being a specialist London dealer. No more has since been heard of it.

Derek Mills-Roberts now lies buried in the Normandy he helped to liberate from German occupation. His ashes are interred beneath an engraved ceramic slab in the village of Bavent, not far from graves elsewhere in the area where other Commandos lie. Bavent is one of a cluster of villages to the east of Caen and the River Orne, taken by First Commando Brigade in the earliest days of the fighting after the Normandy landings and held for several weeks subsequently, until the Allied advance moved on.

Soon after the burial of Mills-Roberts' ashes, his widow Jill described to me in a letter how the villagers of Bavent had arranged a special service in the village church which she and members of her family attended, together with many of the local people as well as a number of surviving Commando veterans. Afterwards there was a modest commemoration, festive rather than sad. 'It was a great day for me, my daughters and my grandchildren,' she wrote. 'Sunshine, lots of flags, laughter at the children marching with the village band, tears at the singing of Auld Lang Syne . . . I have been to Normandy many times. They still maintain Derek's last resting place. They do not forget.'

# MEN OF THE MIDDLE EAST

Jafaa'r Bebehanian (and Others)

# JAFAA'R BEBEHANIAN (AND OTHERS)

## 'In the Days of the Shah . . .'

Some years ago I read *Shah of Shahs*, a book by the Polish journalist Ryszard Kapuscinski whose work was previously unknown to me. It was compelling stuff. Not only did he depict the last member of the Pahlavi dynasty with clarity (Shah Mohammed Reza was cruel, proud, and in many ways stupid); he also told how the Shah inherited a barefoot, semi-literate country which he tried to turn into a sophisticated Western-style power with the aid of vast oil riches but, as we all know, ultimately failed in the process. His reign, until he was finally toppled, was backed by Savak, the ubiquitous secret police who killed, tortured and imprisoned thousands of people in order to enforce the regime.

In one particular passage Kapuscinski referred to an unseemly scramble by Western businessmen to secure lucrative orders and contracts from the Shah's government. It was in the early 1970s, a time when Iran's oil revenues were beginning to quadruple in value and soar to twenty billion dollars a year. He wrote of 'pushing and shoving in the waiting rooms of even the most petty Iranian ministers' by heads of multinational corporations and other representatives of famous companies. It reminded me of a business visit I made myself to Iran in 1958, although the actual circumstances were rather different.

I was then working for Cementation, the London-based civil engineering company, and I had gone to Teheran to set up publicity for two major contracts that it had secured – the construction of a bridge at Khorramshar, in southern Iran, linking the oilfield island of Abadan with the mainland; and the building and fitting-out of a large Hilton hotel in

87

Teheran itself.

Together with Cementation's Middle East manager, Paul Massarik, I first called upon the high-ranking Iranian official who was in effect Cementation's client. He was Administrator-General of the Royal Estates, which covered one-sixth of the entire country, including the land upon which we were proposing to build. His name was Jafaa'r Bebehanian and he was addressed as 'Your Excellency'. He lived in a palace on the outskirts of Teheran.

One morning Paul and I were summoned to see him at the palace and we travelled there in a hired Cadillac so as to create a suitable impression. We found the marble-pillared corridors of the palace crowded with businessmen and favour-seekers, Western and Iranian, and wondered how long we should have to wait. It became apparent that we had been put at the head of the queue, however, and so we were ushered into Bebehanian's lavishly furnished office, where luxurious Persian carpets covered the floor. His desk was at the far end of the room, about sixty feet beyond the tall double doors through which we entered.

As Bebehanian rose from his desk to receive us, a paunchy yet powerfully-built man with close-cropped white hair and heavily-lidded eyes, he reminded me strongly of Sydney Greenstreet, the Hollywood actor renowned for his sinister roles. It was a feeling that never entirely left me. In conversation he displayed a clear grasp of publicity techniques and a familiarity with the organisation of Europe's press, TV and radio that I found surprising. He left me in no doubt about the sort of editorial coverage he expected to see in return for the award of construction work to Cementation. It was to help project the modern Iran, and it was to be extensive.

When our discussion was over Bebehanian waved his hand with a faintly courteous smile and indicated that we should leave. Paul and I both rose from our seats in front of his desk, bowed to him, and walked three paces backwards as protocol demanded. We then turned to start walking from the room and, as we did so, we looked straight into the eyes of two hard-looking young Iranians, their hands on shoulder-holsters inside their jackets, who were sitting no more than ten feet away. They got to their feet and followed us once we had resumed walking. When we reached the double doors at the far end of the room we found that they were locked and we could not get out. Bebehanian swiftly unlocked them by means of a remote control button on his desk – apologising to us as he did so. We learned later that he was terrified of assassination. The two young men who had silently watched us unobserved during our interview with Bebehanian were, of course, Savak agents.

I had one more encounter with Savak before leaving the country. As I was boarding the plane for London at Teheran airport another young plain-clothes policeman came running up the aircraft steps and demanded to see my passport. I handed it to him. He scrutinised it for fully one minute, keeping me standing beside him as other passengers eased past us to get on board. Then, abruptly and without comment, he handed my passport back and allowed me to proceed without further hindrance. What the purpose of it all was I had no idea. Perhaps Bebehanian, I told myself, wanted to make quite sure that I would remember his publicity 'requests' and act upon them with redoubled effort. But I never really knew. Back in London, I managed to obtain a good deal of publicity for the two Cementation contracts – largely because they were good export stories, and the Press were quite keen on getting hold of good stories about British industrial successes overseas at the time. As regards Bebehanian, I neither saw nor heard of him again.

# MEDIA PEOPLE

Eric Baume

Basil Cardew

Howard Marshall

Edward R. Murrow

# ERIC BAUME (1901 – 1967)

## Charisma from Down Under

When Eric Baume died I was surprised to read in a British newspaper that he was Australia's best-known radio commentator. I had known and worked for him many years before, in the early 1940s, when he was London editor of the *Sydney Daily Mirror*. At that time he was essentially a newspaperman. The days of radio fame had yet to come.

I first met Eric in 1942, when he recruited me from the *Daily Sketch* to work in the *Mirror*'s London offices as a junior.

The offices were located in Reuters building at the bottom end of Fleet Street, near Ludgate Circus. The news staff was small and friendly, about a dozen people in all, mainly Australian and British. We worked together in a single large room, with Eric and his secretary in a smaller room adjoining. Our job was to gather, write and transmit several thousand words of news each night via Cable & Wireless to Sydney, in time for the paper's afternoon editions. We also wrote 'mailers' – short feature stories – for later dispatch to Australia by airmail.

Eric himself was a charismatic figure: tall, broad-shouldered, with dark wavy hair and strong features. He was a Jew of Hungarian descent, born of emigré parents in New Zealand. At the age of twenty-two when he was a young married man with three children he moved to Australia – he hated staying in one place for very long. A born gambler with a weakness for the poker tables, he grew up among like-minded Australian newsmen and learned the craft of journalism in a hard school during the Depression years. By the beginning of the war he was one of Australia's top journalists. He was posted to London and moved into the Savoy

Hotel, living in style and never walking anywhere if he could possibly take a taxi – even from Savoy Place to Fleet Street. He also chain-smoked extravagantly, lighting and stubbing out his cigarettes in quick succession.

As a journalist he was basically a hard-hitter, reporting in simple and dramatic terms to a receptive tabloid readership in Australia. Much of the *Sydney Mirror*'s space was devoted to sport and crime, although Eric, in his role of London editor, liked best at that time to write, pundit-style, on political affairs and strategic aspects of the war. ('Baume's Beam' was the title of his regular weekly commentary.) Between times he taught me personally a good deal about 'human interest' reporting, exhorting me always to look for some unexpected, eye-catching angle. One Christmas he sent me out to find and write a Christmas special – 'something unusual, something different'. I came back to the office the following day and told him about a Christmas midnight mass I had attended in a Catholic suburban church: standing in the middle of the packed congregation a young Belgian soldier had suddenly unsheathed the bayonet at his waist and held it high above his head with both hands, hilt uppermost, like a gleaming steel crucifix. 'That's the story,' Eric said enthusiastically. 'Write it, write it.'

Not long after I had joined the *Sydney Mirror* another new member of staff arrived. She introduced herself as Margaret Stewart. Eric had brought her in to write a weekly social column.

Her full name was Lady Margaret Vane-Tempest-Stewart. She was the second daughter of the seventh Marquess of Londonderry. Her mother, the formidable Marchioness Edith, had been London's greatest pre-war political hostess, famous for the brilliance of her large-scale Eve-of-Parliament parties at Londonderry House (Margaret's birthplace) in Park Lane.

When Margaret first arrived in the office it was obvious that she hardly knew one end of a typewriter from the other. But she soon learned, and her social contacts were such that she could hardly fail to impress her women readers in Sydney. More intriguing to us, although it was not really any of our business, was the fact that she and Eric were lovers. They were living together at the Savoy.

Margaret was slim, attractive, in her early thirties, possessed of quiet charm and an easy, outgoing manner. We all liked her a lot, and as we got to know her better we learned from various sources more and more about her. She was extraordinarily accomplished: an excellent horsewoman and rifle shot, a good tennis player, a 'natural' pilot who managed to fly solo after only a few hours' instruction. She was also a talented painter. With Eric's help she eventually became an accredited war correspondent for the paper, reporting the fighting in Normandy in 1944. The following year she crossed the Rhine with the Allied forces – the first woman reporter to do so. By that time I was in uniform myself, serving in Normandy and later taking part in the Rhine assault operation. Our paths in the theatre of war never crossed, however.

In mid-1946, soon after my demob, I returned to the *Sydney Mirror* in London. Other than the fact that the office had moved from Reuters to another building on the other side of Fleet Street, nothing had changed. The same old faces were still there, and Eric was still in vigorous, flamboyant charge. Margaret, too, had returned from the war, looking much the same as when I had last seen her over three years before.

Late in September, the office was heavily involved in covering the Heath murder case, one of the most horrific of the immediate postwar period. Neville George Clevely Heath was a confidence trickster and psychopath, violently sadistic and fatally attractive to women. Aged twenty-nine, he had a ten-year criminal record behind him. He had served in the Army, the RAF and the South African Air Force – gaining, almost unbelievably, a commission in each of them and then being subsequently cashiered for dishonourable conduct.

In the summer of 1946 he committed two murders in rapid succession – the first in Bayswater, west London, and the second in Bournemouth. His first victim, a club hostess named Margery Gardner, was savagely beaten with a steel-tipped riding whip and suffocated; his second, a young ex-Wren named Doreen Marshall, was stripped, stabbed, then finally put to death by having her throat cut.

The two murders took place within days of each other. Heath was quickly discovered and arrested and the resultant Press reports immediately aroused sensational interest, as much in Australia as in Britain. The *Sydney Mirror* instructed us to cable maximum coverage of Heath's trial when it began and also as many background stories as possible, including interviews with relatives and acquaintances of Heath and his family. Eric promptly turned everyone in the office on to the assignment, some going to the Old Bailey to cover the actual trial and the rest of us elsewhere.

I found myself in Wimbledon, seeking an interview with Heath's mother – 'Don't come back until you've got it,' Eric had said. Mrs Heath lived with her husband, a City hairdresser, in a small house in Ridgway, a quiet road at the top of Wimbledon Hill. Although she refused to see any of the newspaper reporters gathered outside the front of her house, I managed to get into her back garden unobserved and after a while to gain her confidence. She was a small, sad woman; quiet, dowdily dressed, modest and unassuming. The Old Bailey trial had begun by the time I met her and she told me that she was not attending it because her son had said that he would plead guilty the moment she entered the courtroom. So she was just carrying on with her normal domestic daily tasks. I went shopping with her on a couple of occasions, smuggling her out of her house the back way and accompanying her to some nearby stores where, mercifully, she attracted no particular attention. Later, back in her home, she showed me various letters written to her by Heath from prison. In all of them he begged her not to attend. 'I want to spare you the horrors,' he had written.

Mrs Heath believed totally in her son's innocence. In the hallway of her house hung a large head-and-shoulders photograph of Heath on the wall. It depicted him as a captain in the South African Air Force with the DFC and other medal ribbons on his breast. 'His mind is not quite right,' she said to me tearfully, after I had told her that he was not in fact a holder of the Distinguished Flying Cross. 'He was recommended for it and probably thought he was fully entitled to it . . . He's a very sick man. I will never lose faith in him.'

In another letter written to his mother from Brixton Prison, Heath emphatically denied killing Margery Gardner. The evidence against him, however, was overwhelmingly conclusive, as he certainly knew. Despite a strong plea of 'moral insanity' mounted by his defence counsel, Heath was sentenced to death for Gardner's murder and duly executed.

A few days before the trial ended, Eric Baume received an unexpected approach. Gardner's estranged husband, a wine salesman by trade and a somewhat shadowy figure, was hawking his wife's memoirs round Fleet Street. No other paper seemed interested in them, but when they were offered to Eric for publication by the *Sydney Mirror* he bought them for £40. The 'memoirs' turned out to be a mediocre collection of disjointed notes, poems and drawings. One of the poems, written by Margery Gardner in 1936, uncannily foretold the manner of her death by flogging and asphyxiation.

Our coverage of the Heath case was splashed in edition after edition of the *Mirror* in Australia, for day after day until there was nothing more to tell. Eric seemed well pleased with the results of our efforts, as were his masters in Sydney. After it was all over we settled down to regular work on more routine stories and features.

Because my future with the paper was clearly limited, I did not stay much longer with Eric. In fact I said my goodbyes to him and to Margaret and to everyone else in the office at the end of 1946 and went to work elsewhere.

I never saw him after that, reading only in the Press that following his return to Sydney after the war he had had a highly successful career in journalism and radio – though not in Australian television, apparently. The final years of his life had been dogged by recurring illness.

I did, however, see Margaret again. It was during the 1960s. I was in Fleet Street one lunch-time and as I was passing one of the bars there I saw her seated alone at a table, a gin and tonic in front of her and smoking as usual. I went in to speak to her and we talked for a while about happenings to both of us since the wartime years. She had aged considerably. Her face was white and drawn, and her hair had darkened. She seemed unhappy. I learned later that she died not long after I had seen her – in October 1966, six months ahead of Eric. She was fifty-six at the time of her death.

# BASIL CARDEW (1906 – 1993)

## A Tale for His Lordship

One of the first recruits to the famous *Daily Express* reporting team of the 1930s was Basil Cardew, an all-rounder from the Press Association news agency, who joined with the reputation of being one of the fastest and most accurate shorthand note-takers in the business.

Under the leadership of Arthur Christiansen, the brilliant editor who had himself been recruited in 1933 by Lord Beaverbrook, the paper's owner, the team transformed the *Express* into the most successful newspaper of the inter-war and immediate postwar years. Through their skills and efforts, sales of the *Express* eventually reached four million copies a day, a record at the time.

A small, dapper man, dressed in a camel-haired coat and wearing a trilby at a rakish angle, Basil exemplified the popular notion of the old-style Fleet Street reporter. He was essentially a sociable character, convivial at the bar and lavish with company expenses. Behind the devil-may-care exterior, however, was a thorough-going professional to whom the story always came first. He was the respected motoring correspondent of the *Express* for many years, and it was in this capacity that I got to know him when I was Head of PR at Ford Motor Company in the early 1960s. We used to have a good deal to do with each other, especially when the pair of us were trying to pin down news information that Sir Patrick Hennessy (Ford's UK chairman and my boss) might have given privately to his great friend Lord Beaverbrook, and for that matter, vice versa.

Among his many other qualities, Basil was a born anecdotalist. This led him one day to tell me of a particular encounter that he once had with his lordship at Beaverbrook's annual tea-party for *Express* staff, given at the Savoy.

Most, if not all, the *Express* staffers went in considerable awe of Beaverbrook, including Basil himself. It was with some mortification, therefore, that he found himself caught nearest to the entrance to the room where the party was being held when his lordship appeared in the doorway. (The other *Express* staffers, displaying more quick-wittedness, had already removed themselves to a safe distance.)

Knowing, as his lordship looked at him, that brief reference to the weather or indeed any other form of small talk would not go down at all well, Basil desperately racked his brains for an interesting item of conversation. He finally remembered something that he thought would be suitable. 'Sir,' he said, 'I heard a rather interesting wartime story about you from a Whitehall friend of mine the other day . . .'

Beaverbrook's eyes narrowed slightly, and he fixed his gaze steadily upon him. 'Tell it, Cardew,' he said.

Basil drew a deep breath. 'It goes like this, sir,' he began. 'When you were Minister of Aircraft Production and attending an important Cabinet meeting, Churchill demanded a definite commitment for one thousand bombers to be produced by our aircraft industry as soon as possible, so that a massive morale-boosting air raid could be mounted on Berlin – the biggest ever.'

'True, Cardew,' commented Beaverbrook in gravelly tones. 'Go on.'

'Well,' resumed Basil, 'You apparently promised the Prime Minister, in response to his urgent request, that you'd personally see to it that our factories produced, within one month, sufficient bombers for the raid – all in a proper state of operational readiness.'

Beaverbrook inclined his head in agreement. 'That is substantially correct, Cardew,' he said. 'Go on.'

'Of course, it wasn't all that easy, was it, sir?' said Basil, warming to his theme. 'I mean, everyone knows what a tremendous effort must have been made, almost superhuman in some cases, all in addition to your own efforts.'

Beaverbrook looked at him silently, half-quizzically, waiting for him to resume once more.

Basil cleared his throat. 'It's at this point, sir, that the story becomes wholly fanciful. The one thousand-bomber raid on Berlin took place within a matter of weeks, as everyone knows. But it's said by some that when the RAF aimers pressed the buttons to release their bombs, hundreds of fitters from the aircraft factories fell out of the planes instead.'

He looked at Beaverbrook somewhat apprehensively. The great man, after a pause, suddenly beamed before walking forward to join the rest of the *Express* partygoers at the other end of the room. 'God bless you, Cardew,' he said. 'A little fanciful, as you say, but as the story epitomises me, continue to tell it.'

# HOWARD MARSHALL (1900 – 1973)

## Britain's Most Famous Voice

When I first met Howard Marshall in 1950 he already had a lifetime of fame behind him. Before the war he had been Britain's most famous radio voice, known to millions for his Test Match commentaries as well as regular broadcasts of many other kinds.

Yet he had long forsaken radio as a career by the time I met him, although he occasionally went back to the microphone when asked to do so. He was specially recalled, for example, to join the team of BBC radio commentators covering the coronation of Queen Elizabeth II in Westminster Abbey in 1953. By then, however, he had been for some years the director of public relations for a large steel company, and it was in this capacity that he interviewed me for a job and very soon afterwards appointed me to his staff. It was the beginning of a friendship that lasted more than twenty years and ended only with his death.

I already knew something about him, of course: indeed, what schoolboy in the 1930s had not listened to his calm, deep voice describing in unhurried tones the drama of the latest Test, or even, as the whole of my school did, the first Royal Wedding to be broadcast? (For the record, it took place in 1934, when Prince George, Duke of Kent, married Princess Marina.)

In his younger days Howard lived for sport. He gained a rugby Blue at Oxford in 1921, won a trial cap for England and also captained the Harlequins. A handsome, imposing man, tall and well-built, his prowess at games extended to cricket where, as a player, he absorbed the technical

101

knowledge that later enabled him to lead the way in cricket broadcasting. He was an accomplished boxer, too.

In 1927 he joined the BBC, then very much an infant organisation. He began as an announcer, but soon found his work, as he put it to me, 'varied and voluminous . . . I drifted about from the News Department to Talks . . . I always seemed to be popping up at a microphone.'

Over the next few years, during which time he did a stint with the *Daily Telegraph* as a special writer mainly on cricket and rugby ('I did it for the money'), radio grew enormously in popularity. He returned to the BBC where 'My broadcasting grew widely . . . cricket came first, I suppose, but I did all kinds of other things, including worldwide Christmas Day programmes, the Epilogue on Sunday evenings, Children's Hour with Uncle Mac, and a series on Britain's slums which brought me 10,000 letters in a week – Other People's Houses, it was called.'

But it was cricket, his broadcast commentaries on the great Test Matches of the 1930s and above all the Test against the Australians in 1938 for which he was most remembered. The Yorkshire batsman Len Hutton, then only twenty-two years old, battled for 13 hours 20 minutes at the Oval over two blazingly hot August days to score 364 for England – the highest score in first-class cricket ever made up to that time. 'I was privileged,' said Howard, recalling the match in a BBC broadcast many years later, 'to describe almost every ball of that innings over the air. Even for a commentator it was something of an endurance test; what it must have been for Hutton out there in the boiling heat I cannot imagine.'

In 1940, soon after the outbreak of war, Howard's career took an unexpected turn. He became director of public relations at the Ministry of Food, advising Lord Woolton, the minister, on how best to win the nation's confidence in matters of food supply and rationing. It was a highly important wartime task which, as a professional communicator, he handled with superb skill and imagination. Years later, one of his former Whitehall colleagues wrote: 'If the Ministry of Food had some success in the war, one of the reasons was Howard Marshall . . . He won the minister and chief civil servant to the view that only if the conduct of the Ministry was good could anyone succeed in getting it the credit . . . that in the sensitive world of food and drink supply, good conduct must include attention, not only to economic and nutritional science, but to the feelings of the public about what they liked and what was fair.'

Behind the scenes at the Ministry, Howard taught Woolton how to handle Press conferences and how to broadcast effectively to the nation. It was all part of a PR director's job, very familiar today, but a rarity then. As a top-level adviser to Woolton and his senior civil servants, Howard was involved in policies and tactics of a sometimes surprising nature. In one instance, so he told me, he found himself engaged in the direction of a propaganda campaign devised as much in the interests of national security as national nutrition. It was at a time in the war, around 1942, when it was crucial to deny the Germans any knowledge of the effectiveness of radar equipment fitted to Britain's night-fighter aircraft. The story was therefore put about that the RAF's pilots owed their success in shooting down enemy planes at night to the fact that carrots formed a valuable part of their diet by enabling them to see more clearly in darkness. The story gained wide credence at the time and helped, if only for a while, to preserve the radar secret; it also helped to persuade the public of carrots' nutritional value.

In 1943 Woolton lost Howard. 'I was taken from the Ministry of Food and made director of war reporting at the BBC,' he told me. It was a job in which he headed a team of war correspondents operating in Northern Europe who became in some instances even better known than he was – Frank Gillard, Chester Wilmot and Wynford Vaughan-Thomas among them. His own greatest wartime broadcast was made on D Day itself, 6 June 1944. After landing that morning on the Normandy beaches he succeeded in getting back to England to give the first eye-witness account on the BBC news, the same evening, of the initial assault by Allied troops. He accomplished this despite his landing-craft 'being sunk and losing all my broadcasting gear . . . and being personally sunk again no less than three times before being finally fished out of the water and given a launch to take me home.'

Together with other BBC correspondents, Howard continued to cover the fighting in Normandy. He was one of the first to broadcast from Paris the following August. ('It's a city of violent contrasts, a city celebrating the entry of the Allies with wild enthusiasm and gaiety, and yet a city still at war, with all its gaiety broken by gun flashes and the rattle of machine guns at street corners.') Another broadcast that he used to recall was his description of a memorial service in the great cathedral of Chartres, held to honour thirty-nine young French resistance men and women who had been killed in the fighting. The Germans were still in the city at the time that he was recording his radio dispatch.

By 1946, with the war ended, Howard was in demand from several quarters. Lord Kemsley, the Press baron, wanted him as Editor-in-Chief of Kemsley national and provincial newspapers; Sir Alexander Korda, the film tycoon, invited him to become publicity chief for Korda Film Productions and to write his own contract. Neither these nor other offers appealed to him, however, and a chance meeting with the industrialist E.H. Lever (later Sir Ernest Lever) led him in a totally different direction. He joined Richard Thomas & Co., the steel company, as an adviser on human relations. Lever, a former head of the Prudential, was chairman of Richard Thomas. At the time he was actively promoting a merger with Baldwins Limited, an old-established Midland steel company whose directors once included Stanley Baldwin.

The merger took place, and Howard's energies were turned towards helping to create amongst the employees of the two companies, formerly bitter competitors, an understanding of the new organisation's aims and policies and a sense of common purpose. With Lever's unwavering support, this was broadly achieved: the human problems that so frequently arise through the mishandling of people in merger situations were largely avoided.

Howard then went on to become director of personnel and public relations for the company, now named Richard Thomas & Baldwins Limited, or RTB for short. As at the Ministry of Food, he held strongly to the principle that good conduct lay at the heart of good PR. ('A company's public relations begins on the inside, with concern for its own people. That's the key to good performance. Taking the credit for it comes later.')

Backed by Ernest Lever, who regularly toured RTB's forty steel and tinplate works in England and South Wales, Howard built up a personnel and PR unit that covered an unusually wide range of functions. His staff included steelworks doctors and nurses, education and training specialists, a catering adviser, Press officers, publicists and other communicators. The last-named included several young journalists who in two or three instances went on to bigger things in Fleet Street. Between them they produced award-winning company newspapers and magazines, and also a company newsreel that was regularly screened in steeltown cinemas across the country.

Such primarily employee-centred activities would no doubt be regarded in business today as smacking too much of 'welfare' and therefore not to be countenanced. But times were different then, and the whole idea worked well. More than one leading company adopted some of Howard's ideas after visiting RTB – to see how it was done.

For many years Howard was a leading member of the Savile Club, where he was chairman of the house committee.

Because his Brook Street office stood just across the road from the Savile he found it convenient to lunch regularly at the Club and from time to time bring one or two of his friends over to see what we were doing. This led to such luminaries as Sir Compton Mackenzie, Gerald Barry and Richard Church being persuaded to write for one of our magazines or (more usually) to address some company conference that Howard was in the process of arranging. His object was to open the minds of people working in RTB to different worlds, and perhaps vice versa.

In 1958, after twelve years' work for the company, Howard was suddenly struck down by an illness that later turned out to be Parkinson's Disease. It was the beginning of a long period of increasing disablement and he was obliged to remain for the most part in his remote Berkshire cottage, struggling up to London by train only on rare occasions. RTB retained his services as an adviser, and I deputised for him in the office. I also used to visit him in Berkshire, where I discovered that he would regularly go for three-mile walks in the countryside, somehow dragging himself along, but always quietly cheerful. He remained, too, a great fisherman, taking himself not only to the banks of a nearby river but also keeping in touch with his friends on the *Angling Times* and *Trout and Salmon* – two journals which, as an acknowledged authority on angling, he had found time earlier in an active life to help launch and write for.

At the time of his death in 1973 *The Times* described him as a man who had snapped his fingers at fame. It was a fair description, one that he would probably have agreed with. It would certainly not have bothered him. He was far too big for that.

# EDWARD R. MURROW (1908 – 1965)

## Awakening America

Early in 1955 I was sent to the States by Howard Marshall, my chief at RTB, to study US television. My assignment was to find out how it operated, and in particular to assess the pros and cons of TV advertising and the commercial sponsorship of programmes. Independent Television was soon to start in Britain (it actually began the following September) and very few people in this country had any conception at the time of the impact that 'commercials' were likely to have upon business or indeed daily life.

One of my first contacts in the US was Edward R. Murrow, the distinguished international reporter and news analyst. Howard Marshall had known Ed Murrow since pre-war days and Murrow, in response to Howard's request, willingly gave me time to meet him and to study his news and programme set-up at CBS.

I was therefore 'attached' to CBS for the best part of a month in New York. I soon realised (it was my first visit to America) that Murrow's weekly TV programmes *See It Now* and *Person to Person*, as well as his daily news commentaries for CBS Radio, commanded immense audiences throughout the country. His prestige was such that he had ready access to leading figures everywhere. 'His name,' a CBS producer said to me, 'is an Open Sesame wherever we go.'

My first meeting with Murrow took place in his office, seventeen floors up in the CBS building on Madison Avenue. It was an unpretentious room, small and workmanlike. Reference books lined the walls, and in one corner stood a chest-high reading desk on which lay copies of the latest US and European newspapers. Murrow himself was in working dress: discarded jacket, loosened tie, white shirt open at the neck. His alert brown eyes harboured a reflective glint, yet when he smiled it was an exceedingly warm and friendly smile. When I told him how much we wanted to learn from American TV, he quickly headed me off. 'There aren't any experts in this business over here,' he said. 'We're still learning, same as everybody else.'

He then switched to questioning me, the visitor from London, about my own particular job and about industrial conditions in Britain. After a while I managed to get him talking again. As he lit yet another cigarette (he smoked over seventy a day) he confided one of his pet television projects to me: a scheme for developing the two-way exchange of TV programmes between Britain and America, under joint Anglo-US sponsorship. 'It's a dream,' he admitted finally, 'but one day it might come true.' (It didn't, of course, not at any rate in the way that Murrow envisioned; but to me at the time it conveyed something of his character as an idealist and dreamer.)

For decades over the air, Murrow's grave, clipped manner of speaking was familiar to millions of households throughout the US. 'He sounds like an unfrocked bishop,' a speech expert once said of him. But the prestige Murrow enjoyed stemmed from pre-war Europe: many Americans still remembered his on-the-spot reporting of the 1938 Anschluss, when Hitler annexed Austria. Fifteen years later, he championed of Robert Oppenheimer, the distinguished physicist suspended from secret nuclear research work by a US security review board – warmly supported by the many people who disagreed strongly with the charges brought against Oppenheimer at the time.

After his devastating exposure of Senator Joseph McCarthy, the rabid anti-communist witch-hunter, on television in 1953, Murrow's political critics dubbed him a Red. If anything, however, he was a man above politics, a genuine seeker after truth.

I certainly felt this when I talked to him. It was clear to me, as to many others, that he stood for the right to present issues and facts as he saw them, and his record as a reporter proved it. He was not concerned, like most other people in the TV industry, with the ratings his programmes got; he was not at all influenced for that matter, or so it seemed to me, by the needs of commercialism. 'If I got involved in the ratings business,' he said to me, 'I might be tempted to hot up what I write. And that's something I never want to do.' So far as anyone could be reasonably objective, therefore, Murrow was. At the same time he was much concerned with the extent to which unconscious prejudices colour a man's thinking. 'We are all,' he once commented, 'prisoners of our own experience.'

In thirty years of reporting for American radio and TV, Murrow covered a fair slice of the world. He interviewed many of the greatest figures of the time, and counted statesmen among his confidantes. President Roosevelt invited him to the White House to tell him privately of the attack on Pearl Harbour in December 1941, hours before the story was officially released. Other world leaders, Churchill among them, were his personal friends. In Murrow's stories of ordinary people, however, an innate sympathy revealed itself. ('I come of working class people and that's where I like to be. When the story of labour is involved, I always go round to the other side of the desk.')

Where Britain was concerned, Murrow displayed an equally unashamed prejudice. He spent nine years here as European director of CBS and as a war correspondent. His measured, gravel-toned 'This is London' became the introductory trademark for his wartime broadcasts to America, in which he reported the London blitz – often from a bomb-blasted rooftop. He played a leading part in awakening America to what was happening in Europe, with Britain standing alone against Hitler's onslaught. His pro-Britishness, which never left him, was such that at one time early in the war he was offered the job of Director-General of the BBC. He declined with regret, but later, in recognition of his support for Britain's cause, he was made an honorary KBE.

Metaphorically speaking, Murrow always kept his suitcase packed. He was ready to travel anywhere, any time, in search of world news. I sat in his office one day when word came through that Pandit Nehru had arrived in London on a short visit and would be prepared to talk to him for his programme *See It Now*. At that time a crisis over Formosa (Taiwan) was uppermost in American-Chinese foreign affairs and Murrow was anxious for Nehru's views. Together with a co-producer he flew to London on the next plane, saw Nehru the following day, and then arrived back in New York with the interview literally in the can. 'We filmed and recorded Nehru for seventy-five minutes,' he told me. 'We got what we wanted.' In these days of instant live interview by satellite, I doubt whether he would have got anything like as much.

Well over a hundred people, among them script editors, producers, cameramen, sound engineers, electricians and publicity men, assisted in the weekly presentation of *See It Now* and Murrow's other TV programme, *Person to Person*. On radio, Murrow also delivered, from Mondays to Fridays, a daily fifteen-minute commentary for CBS News.

The Murrow machine, as it was sometimes termed, was formidably efficient and in every sense at the leading edge of the technology of the day. While the film cameras of *See It Now* scouted whole continents for newsworthy material, the *Person to Person* team quietly prepared, at a smooth but relentless pace, arrangements for interviews in every part of America for live transmission – weeks in advance of actual requirement.

In each edition of *Person to Person*, which ran for thirty minutes, Murrow in his New York studio would take his audience into the homes of two different celebrities, often thousands of miles apart. In his choice of personalities he always sought balance through contrast, and above all to keep the viewers guessing as to who they were likely to see. He once 'paired' the Washington socialite Mrs Perle Mesta with Broadway comedian Bert Lahr, and many of his other combinations were equally unexpected. His selections, which included hundreds of people over the years, ranged from Ethel Barrymore and Bob Hope to ex-President Harry Truman, Mrs Eleanor Roosevelt and the Duke and Duchess of Windsor.

I went out with a *Person to Person* crew the week that Murrow had selected Garry Moore (a well known American comedian) to be 'paired' with *Forever Amber* novelist Kathleen Winsor. During the afternoon of the day of transmission an advance party of cameramen, electricians and sound engineers travelled thirty miles out of New York to Garry

Moore's family home at Rye in Westchester county. By the time I arrived that evening with other members of the crew the front of the house was bathed in the light of arc lamps and the grounds were full of parked vehicles, including a large 'remote' truck used for outside broadcasts. A 90-foot steel tower had also been erected behind the house to microwave the TV picture direct to CBS New York.

Inside the house, miles of cable had been taped to the walls, whilst microphones had been concealed everywhere. Carpets had been rolled back and furniture re-arranged to suit the best camera angles. A technical rehearsal was in progress, with members of the crew busily moving cameras, lights and sound equipment from one position to another. In the nearby kitchen a cook was making pots of hot coffee and piles of sandwiches for everyone. The Moore family – Garry, his wife and their two young sons – quietly watched the hurried activity going on all around them with complete equanimity. Similar rapid preparations, as I saw on the monitor screens in the 'remote' truck outside, were being made in Kathleen Winsor's Manhattan apartment.

At 10.30 p.m. precisely, the show went on the air. Murrow's smiling face appeared upon the screen. 'Good evening. I'm Ed Murrow. The name of the programme is *Person to Person*. It's all live – there's no film. Once again tonight we'll be doing a little informal visiting. First to the penthouse of novelist Kathleen Winsor, here in New York, and then up to Rye, the home of the Garry Moores.'

The scene changed to a shot of Murrow looking out of a window from his studio chair. Across the street, as it were, was a large apartment block. The cameras took the programme's 12 million viewers through the window to the elegant interior of Miss Winsor's lounge. 'Come on in, Ed,' she smiled. And we all went in with him.

'Do you find writing fun?' Murrow asked. Miss Winsor, as elegant as her apartment, said yes, she found it exhilarating – 'But it's one thing to say you're going to write a best-seller, and another to do it.' It had taken, she said, 4,967 hours to write *Forever Amber* (a sensationally successful bonkbuster at the time) and she was now planning to write another historical novel for which she had already researched 120 books. 'Getting back to *Forever Amber*, Kay,' interposed Murrow, 'were you surprised at how well it was received?' Miss Winsor demurely replied that she certainly was. 'I wrote it like a textbook, but the critics said Wow.'

Whether he was interviewing celebrities on *Person to Person* or delivering a carefully considered commentary on *See It Now*, Ed Murrow was primarily a reporter. By British standards he could sometimes seem a touch melodramatic – especially when watched on TV in Britain, divorced from the frenetic overtones of New York. Yet this could never seriously detract from the fact that he was by common consent a great reporter – perhaps the greatest America has ever produced.

My 'attachment' to CBS did not by any means constitute the whole of my study of American TV in the mid-1950s. I spent a good deal of time with United States Steel and other leading industrial corporations to see how they made use of TV as an advertising and promotional medium, and what they got out of it; but I learned more about American television from Ed Murrow and his team than I learned from anyone else. And I also had more fun.